Amazing Doctrines

Essential Bible Truths
for Sharing Your Faith

A 13-Week Lesson Book Presented by the
Amazing Facts Center of Evangelism

Amazing Doctrines

Published by Amazing Facts International
P.O. Box 1058
Roseville, CA 95678
916-434-3880
www.afbookstore.com

Written by Kristyn Dolinsky, Daniel Hudgens, Laurie Lyon, Carissa McSherry, Carlos Muñoz, Curtis Rittenour, Joelle Worf
Edited by Michelle Kiss

Cover and interior design by Daniel Hudgens
Layout by Greg Solie • Altamont Graphics

ISBN 978-1-58019-608-6

Table of Contents

FOREWORD

If you were stranded on a deserted island, what would you need to survive? What would you consider to be essential equipment? Besides water, food, and shelter, many survivalists would add a knife, fishing net, and box of matches. Of course, it also would be nice to have an inflatable raft, a flashlight, sunblock, and a satellite phone!

But I would add one more essential item: a Bible. Nothing is more important to survival in our world than the Word of God. It keeps us connected with the Source of life, the Bread and the Living Water. It reminds us that we can "abide under the shadow of the Almighty" (Psalm 91:1). And when you are in trouble, deliverance "from the snare of the fowler and from the perilous pestilence" (v. 2).

Amazing Doctrines is an essential tool to equip you with the basic teachings of Scripture, not only to bolster your own faith, but also to provide you with indispensable knowledge to share with others. In one sense, we are all stranded on a sin-filled island called Earth and are in need of God's truth to rescue us from Satan's snares.

God bless your journey through *Amazing Doctrines*. May you be "thoroughly equipped for every good work" (2 Timothy 3:17).

Doug Batchelor, President
Amazing Facts International

INTRODUCTION

Welcome to *Amazing Doctrines*! This powerful equipping manual focuses on essential Bible teachings for Christians living in these last days. This compact study consists of 13-weeks of lessons that will give you a deeper grasp of Bible doctrines in order to strengthen your faith and prepare you to share it with others.

There is a trend today among Christians to react negatively to the word "doctrine." One common refrain is, "We need Jesus not doctrine!" While it's true that we need Jesus, we should remember that Jesus and doctrine actually go hand in hand.

The first mention of doctrine in the Bible comes from the Lord, who said, "My doctrine shall drop as the rain, my speech shall distil as the dew, as the small rain upon the tender herb, and as the showers upon the grass" (Deuteronomy 32:2 KJV). The word doctrine simply means teaching or instruction.

Notice what the Bible says about Jesus: "When Jesus had ended these sayings, the people were astonished at his doctrine" (Matthew 7:28 KJV). Jesus also said, 'I am the way, the truth, and the life. No one comes to the Father except through Me'" (John 14:6).

Therefore, doctrine is biblical teaching that defines the way to Christ and is always centered in Jesus. "Whoever transgresses and does not abide in the doctrine of Christ does not have God. He who abides in the doctrine of Christ has both the Father and the Son" (2 John 1:9).

Ellen White beautifully captures this truth:

"The Sacrifice of Christ as an atonement for sin is the great truth around which all other truths cluster. In order to be rightly understood and appreciated, every truth in the Word of God, from Genesis to Revelation, must be studied in the light that streams from the cross of Calvary. I present before you the great, grand monument of mercy and regeneration, salvation and redemption—the Son of God uplifted on the cross. This is to be the foundation of every discourse given by our ministers" (*Gospel Workers*, p. 315).

Keep these thoughts central as you go through these lessons, because the devil wants to distort the pure doctrines of the Scriptures and replace them with his own. Jesus warned the Pharisees, "Hypocrites! Well did Isaiah prophesy about you, saying: 'These people draw near to Me with their mouth, and honor Me with their lips, but their heart is far from Me. And in vain they worship Me, teaching as doctrines the commandments of men'" (Matthew 15:7–9).

May God bless you as you start *Amazing Doctrines*!

Carlos Muñoz, Director
Amazing Facts Center of Evangelism

Chapter One
SCRIPTURE

The Foundation of Our Faith

Her bare feet scuffed against the old dirt path. Mile after mile she trudged, undaunted by the dangers or hardship.

For eight long years, Mary Jones had scrimped and saved to buy the object she desired most—a Bible in her own language. Born in Wales to underprivileged Calvinistic Methodist parents, Mary yearned from a young age to study the Bible for herself. After eight years of saving, fifteen-year-old Mary received news that Bibles were available for purchase in a town 26 miles away. Without hesitation, she excitedly began her long journey.

Upon hearing of this young girl's devotion and dedication, Reverend Thomas Charles was so inspired that he soon created the British and Foreign Bible Society, empowering countless others to receive Bibles of their own. Since its inception in 1804, millions of Bibles have been distributed worldwide, all because of a young girl and a very long journey.

What is it about the Bible that is so intriguing? From a young age, many are told to merely accept Scripture at face value and to believe it unquestionably. But is this what God wants? Can the Bible be tested? What is the evidence for believing what it says? Join us as we explore these questions and more!

Hide Them in Your Heart
Memorize the following verses this week!

"All Scripture is given by inspiration of God, and is profitable for doctrine, for reproof, for correction, for instruction in righteousness, that the man of God may be complete, thoroughly equipped for every good work." —2 Timothy 3:16, 17

"Sanctify them by Your truth. Your word is truth." —John 17:17

God Is Big Enough for Your Questions

Read: Acts 17:10, 11

React: In the estimation of the apostles, what made the Bereans noble? How can we apply these principles in our study of the Bible and in what we hear from religious leaders?

_____

_____

_____

How do you respond when your word is questioned? Naturally, we are prone to be defensive, expecting others to believe us simply because we say something is true. However, this was not the approach of the apostles; they applauded questions and the willingness of seekers to search the Scriptures for themselves.

Likewise, in Isaiah 1:18, God Himself states, "Come now, and let us reason together." The Lord invites us to conversation, to ask questions, and to prove for ourselves "whether these things were so" (Acts 17:11).

Read: Matthew 4:4, 7, 10; John 17:17; Luke 24:27

React: How did Jesus demonstrate His belief in the Scriptures?

_____

_____

_____

Shortly before His unjust trial and crucifixion, Jesus passionately prayed these words to His Father: "Sanctify them by Your truth. Your word is truth" (John 17:17). In the midst of painful lies and scathing accusations, Jesus knew He could grasp onto the Word of God because it would never fail Him. So also today, in a world filled with facades and deceit, God's Word remains true.

Reflection and Discussion: Read Matthew 22:37. What does it mean to love the Lord with all your mind? How can this verse be applied in our daily lives?

_____

_____

_____

Socrates, the famed Greek philosopher, once said, "The unexamined life is not worth believing." Today we could truly say, "The unexamined faith is not worth living."[1] It is crucial that we know both *what* we believe and *why* we believe it. Just as Joshua of old called the Israelites to "choose for yourselves this day whom you will serve" (Joshua 24:15), we too are called to make an educated decision for God.

1   N. L. Geisler and F. Turek, *I Don't Have Enough Faith to Be an Atheist* (Wheaton, IL: Crossway, 2004), pg. 29

Can I Get a Witness?

The Bible boldly claims, "All Scripture is given by inspiration of God" (2 Timothy 3:16). Many accept this declaration at face value, but can it be proven true? How do we know if the Bible is indeed a credible source?

Read: Isaiah 46:9, 10; John 14:29

React: What claims does God make about Himself? If proven true, how do these claims lend credibility to the Scriptures?

_____

_____

_____

Accurately predicting the future is one way of quickly building credibility. Does the Bible do this? Some examples of this are the fulfilled prophecies in the book of Daniel, specifically chapters 2, 7, 8, and 9. Written more than 500 years before Christ, the prophecies of Daniel 2 span some 2,500 years and have been fulfilled with amazing accuracy! (See Amazing Facts Study Guide #1.) In addition, consider the following Messianic prophecies.

Prophecy		Old Testament Prediction	New Testament Fulfillment
1.	Born in Bethlehem	Micah 5:2	Matthew 2:1
2.	Born of a virgin	Isaiah 7:14	Matthew 1:18–23
3.	David's lineage	Jeremiah 23:5	Revelation 22:16
4.	Target of murder attempt	Jeremiah 31:15	Matthew 2:16-18
5.	Betrayed by a friend	Psalm 41:9	John 13:18, 19, 26
6.	Sold for 30 silver coins	Zechariah 11:12	Matthew 26:14–16
7.	Crucified	Zechariah 12:10	John 19:16-18, 37
8.	Lots cast for His clothes	Psalm 22:18	Matthew 27:35
9.	No bones broken	Psalm 34:20	John 19:31-36
10.	Buried in rich man's tomb	Isaiah 53:9	Matthew 27:57–60
11.	Year, day, hour of His death	Daniel 9:26, 27; Exodus 12:6	Matthew 27:45–50
12.	Raised the third day	Hosea 6:2	Acts 10:38–40

There are over 125 messianic prophecies recorded in Scripture. What are the odds that Jesus could have fulfilled just eight of these prophecies by mere chance? Dr. Peter Stoner, former chairman of the departments of mathematics, astronomy, and engineering at Pasadena College in California, applied the principle of probability to this question. He calculated the odds of just eight being fulfilled by one man as one in 1,000,000,000,000,000,000,000,000,000,000!

Read: Revelation 1:1–3

React: Who is the focus of prophecy? Why is it crucial to never lose this focus? And what promises are given to those who read, hear, and keep these things?

_____

_____

_____

Martin Luther once said, "The Bible is the cradle wherein Christ is laid." While the Bible does reveal crucial information about the Antichrist, earth's world powers, and last-day events, it is paramount that we never lose the true focus—the Lamb, Jesus Christ.

A Trustworthy Foundation

Read: Luke 24:13–27

React: How did Jesus substantiate His role as the Messiah to these seekers of truth? Why did He point them to Scripture instead of immediately revealing His identity?

_____

_____

_____

Imagine that, after a tragic case of mistaken identity, your family is led to believe that you have died. Later, you enter your home and are surprised to find your family grieving in deep despair. How would you respond? "I'm here! I'm alive! I'm not dead!" would be a natural response for most.

Jesus, on the other hand, took the time to deepen and affirm their faith in the Scriptures first. He did not desire their faith to be founded solely upon the sand of feeling or experience, but instead upon the unfailing rock of Scripture.

And for good reason. The Bible is unique; it's not just another book. Consider the following interesting facts:

- Written in three languages, over a 1,500-year span, on three continents.

- Has more than forty authors, including kings, military leaders, peasants, philosophers, fishermen, tax collectors, poets, musicians, statesmen, scholars, and shepherds.

- Has a wide variety of literary styles—poetry, historical narrative, song, romance, personal correspondence, biography, autobiography, law, prophecy, and parables.

- Despite all these different elements, it tells a single unfolding story with a lead character—Christ.

- It is the most translated book in history. According to United Bible Societies, the Bible has been translated into more than 2,200 languages, which represent the primary vehicle of communication for well over 90 percent of the world's population.

- Archeological discoveries are continually proving the historical accuracy of the Bible. For years, skeptics said that the Bible was unreliable because it mentions the Hittite nation (Deuteronomy 7:1) and cities like Nineveh (Jonah 1:1, 2) and Sodom (Genesis 19:1), which they denied ever existed. They also claimed that the biblical record of Moses was not reliable because it mentions writing (Exodus 24:4) and wheeled vehicles (Exodus 14:25), neither of which they said existed at the time. But modern archeology has confirmed all of these biblical statements.

- It is well documented. John Warwick Montgomery, a professor of philosophy and law, affirmed: "To be skeptical of the resultant text of the New Testament books is to allow all of classical antiquity to slip into obscurity, for no documents of the ancient period are so well attested bibliographically as the New Testament."

The Essence of Scripture

Read: Romans 15:4; John 15:11; John 14:29; John 17:3

React: Why was Scripture written? How does it affect our lives?

_____

_____

_____

While many in Christ's day had a cerebral knowledge of the Scriptures, they did not have a saving relationship with Him because that knowledge had not sunk into their hearts. We may have all the answers, we may know all the Scriptures, but unless we allow God to use His Word to transform our lives, those things are worth nothing. (See 1 Corinthians 13.)

Revelation is the process by which Divinity communicates with man. There are two types of revelation: general and specific.

General revelation can include:

- Nature: Such as Moses' burning bush or nature declaring the glory of God (Psalm 19:1; Romans 1:20)

- Human experience: Such as miraculously surviving a car accident

- Conscience or reason

However, none of these revelations in and of themselves are complete revelations. There are other religions that look to nature but have a very misconstrued image of God. This is why we have Scripture and the prophets.

In speaking to the Athenians, the apostle Paul commented on their idol to the "unknown God" (Acts 17:23). How can this God be known? We can know the Lord through specific revelation, which are direct messages from the Bible itself and the prophets through whom God spoke.

These specific messages are just as important to our lives today as they were two thousand years ago. Charles Spurgeon once said, "Nobody ever outgrows Scripture; the book widens and deepens with our years." Sometimes we feel content splashing around in the kiddie pool, positioned right beside the ocean's shore. God is calling us to dive deeper into His inexhaustible Word.

Reflection and Discussion: Read John 10:10. What other evidence reveals the power of God?

_____

_____

_____

Your Questions Answered

Q. Is all of the Bible inspired—or just parts of it?

A. "All Scripture is given by inspiration of God, and is profitable for doctrine, for reproof, for correction, for instruction in righteousness" (2 Timothy 3:16). The Bible does not merely contain the words of God—it is the Word of God.

Q. Many brilliant people in the world believe that no one can understand the Bible. If it is truly God's book, shouldn't everyone be able to understand it?

A. Bright people who can understand virtually anything else are often quickly perplexed when they read the Bible. The reason is because spiritual things "are spiritually discerned" (1 Corinthians 2:13, 14). The deep things of the Word will never be understood by a worldly mind, no matter how brilliant. Unless one honestly seeks an experience with God, he or she cannot understand the things of God. The Holy Spirit, who explains the Bible (John 14:26; 16:13), is not understood by the secular mind. On the other hand, the humble, even the uneducated, seeker who studies the Bible receives amazing understanding from the Holy Spirit (Matthew 11:25; 1 Corinthians 2:9, 10).

Firm Foundation

"At last count, there are nearly 5,700 handwritten Greek manuscripts of the New Testament. In addition, there are more than 9,000 manuscripts in other languages. Some of these nearly 15,000 manuscripts are complete Bibles, others are books or pages, and a few are just fragments. ... There is nothing from the ancient world that even comes close in terms of manuscript support. The new closest work is the Iliad by Homer, with 643 manuscripts. Most other ancient works survive on fewer than a dozen manuscripts, yet few historians question the historicity of the events those works describe" (Geisler and Turek, 2004).

"As no other reliable history dates so far back as the Bible, we are obliged to look mainly to its own internal evidence, as to its origin, authorship, and the reason for its existence, and indeed for its credibility in every respect; and further, we should look for such corroboration of its statements as reason, its own harmony with itself, and with other known facts, and subsequent developments furnish. And indeed this is the evidence of reliability on which all history must rest. To such evidence we are indebted for all our knowledge of past events and of all present events as well, except such as come under our own immediate observation. He who would cast away Bible history as unworthy of credence, must on the same ground reject all history; and to be entirely consistent, must believe nothing which does not come under his own personal observation. If its statements, thoroughly understood, are contradictory, or are colored by prejudice, or are proven untrue by a positive scientific knowledge, or if subsequent developments prove its predictions untrue, and thereby show the ignorance or dishonesty of the authors of the Bible, then we may reasonably conclude that the entire book is unworthy of confidence, and should reject it. But if, on the contrary, we find that a thorough understanding of the Bible, according to its own rules of interpretation, shows its statements to be in harmony with each other; if it bears no evidence of prejudicial coloring; if many of its prophecies have actually come true, and others admit of future fulfillment; if the integrity of its writers is manifested by unvarnished records, then we have reason to believe the book. Its entire testimony, historic, prophetic, and doctrinal, stands or falls together" (Geisler and Nix, 1974).

Lesson Summary

1. God invites our questions.
2. Prophecy, science, and archeology give evidence for the authenticity and trustworthiness of Scripture.
3. It is the presence of God, not knowledge alone, which transforms our lives.
4. The core of prophecy is Jesus Christ.

Chapter Two
SALVATION, PART 1

The Origin of Evil

A young boy stands with his fist clenched, shaking it toward the heavens. As the tears pour down his cheeks, his body trembles with emotion.

He strains his vocal cords yelling the question that has haunted every human who has ever lived: "Why?" Why had his mother lost the battle to cancer? Why wasn't she healed? Why did she have to suffer? What did she do to ever deserve such a terrible end? Without answers, these questions would traumatize his heart and mind for the rest of his life.

It isn't hard to empathize with him; is it? You don't need a vivid imagination to realize that something just isn't right about our world. When we survey the tragedy filling up the world and the heartbreaking events in our own lives, we can echo his questions. And we can distill all these questions down to one ultimate inquiry: Why is there evil?

The bad news is that too many bad things are happening to too many good people. Humanity seems to be filled with hatred and violence, and it seems to be getting worse by the day.

But there is also good news. We don't have to keep asking. The Bible provides vital answers to our toughest question. Get ready to discover this week the origin of evil and God's comforting solution to the problem.

Hide Them in Your Heart

Memorize the following verses this week!

"You are of your father the devil, and the desires of your father you want to do. He was a murderer from the beginning, and does not stand in the truth, because there is no truth in him. When he speaks a lie, he speaks from his own resources, for he is a liar and the father of it." —John 8:44

"He who sins is of the devil, for the devil has sinned from the beginning. For this purpose the Son of God was manifested, that He might destroy the works of the devil." —1 John 3:8

The Golden Rule of Heaven

Read: *Patriarchs and Prophets*, p. 35.

> So long as all created beings acknowledged the allegiance of love, there was perfect harmony throughout the universe of God. It was the joy of the heavenly host to fulfill the purpose of their Creator. They delighted in reflecting His glory and showing forth His praise. And while love to God was supreme, love for one another was confiding and unselfish.

React: What preserved perfect harmony in heaven?

_____

_____

_____

Love made perfect harmony in heaven possible. But we often throw the word "love" around without much consideration for its true meaning. For instance, we might say, "I *love* that shirt," or, "I *love* mashed potatoes."

But biblical love is defined as unselfish, benevolent concern for the good of another—like the fatherly care that God has for humankind. The apostle John, who learned something about love as Jesus' disciple, wrote, "He who does not love does not know God, for God is love" (1 John 4:8).

Read: Isaiah 14:12–14; Ezekiel 28:13–17; *Patriarchs and Prophets*, p. 35.

> There was no note of discord to mar the celestial harmonies. But a change came over this happy state. There was one who perverted the freedom that God had granted to His creatures. Sin originated with him who, next to Christ, had been most honored of God and was highest in power and glory among the inhabitants of heaven. Lucifer, "son of the morning," was first of the covering cherubs, holy and undefiled. He stood in the presence of the great Creator, and the ceaseless beams of glory enshrouding the eternal God rested upon him.

React: What was Lucifer's position in God's kingdom? What happened in his heart that caused him to change?

_____

_____

_____

17

Lucifer's role was as covering cherub. The Hebrew word for "covering" is *sâkak*, which can mean "to protect." The name "Lucifer" is often translated as "light bearer" in Scripture. Thus, it appears that Lucifer's role was to "protect" the glory of God by reflecting the love of the Creator to the rest of the universe.

However, Lucifer apparently got caught up in his own beauty, talents, and the respect other angels gave to him. He began putting his desire for further exaltation above even the One who created him. Lucifer set out to eclipse the light of God and convince the angelic host to worship him instead.

Reflection and Discussion: Read this selection from *The Great Controversy*, pg. 495.

Pride in his own glory nourished the desire for supremacy. The high honors conferred upon Lucifer were not appreciated as the gift of God and called forth no gratitude to the Creator. He gloried in his brightness and exaltation, and aspired to be equal with God. He was beloved and reverenced by the heavenly host. Angels delighted to execute his commands, and he was clothed with wisdom and glory above them all. Yet the Son of God was the acknowledged Sovereign of heaven, one in power and authority with the Father. In all the councils of God, Christ was a participant, while Lucifer was not permitted thus to enter into the divine purposes. "Why," questioned this mighty angel, "should Christ have the supremacy? Why is He thus honored above Lucifer?"

Does your desire for advancement at work or in the church sometimes cloud the role you have already been given? Pray that the Lord gives you a heart for service.

The Real Star Wars

God's government included not only the inhabitants of heaven, but of all the worlds that He had created; and Satan thought that if he could carry the angels of heaven with him in rebellion, he could carry also the other worlds. He had artfully presented his side of the question, employing sophistry and fraud to secure his objects. His power to deceive was very great, and by disguising himself in a cloak of falsehood he had gained an advantage. Even the loyal angels could not fully discern his character or see to what his work was leading (*The Great Controversy*, pg. 497).

Genuine love respects the freedom of each individual to reject or accept that love. Thus, even as Lucifer's selfishness became more malignant, God's character of love allowed the angel to spread his ideas to the rest of the universe. However, in order to accomplish his purposes, Lucifer used outright lies and deception.

Read: Revelation 12:7–9; Luke 10:18

React: What happened in heaven as a consequence of Lucifer's deceptions? By what names is the fallen angel called today—and what do these names mean?

_____

_____

_____

Stars in biblical prophetic language symbolize angels. Revelation 12:4 reveals that Lucifer's lies successfully led a third of the angels into full-blown rebellion against God—a rebellion that continues to this day. No longer a "light bearer" of God's love, Lucifer was renamed Satan, which means "adversary," and the devil, which means "slanderer." The angels who followed Satan are called demons.

Read: Job 1:6, 7; 2:1, 2; Revelation 12:12; 1 Peter 5:8

React: What do the passages in Job reveal about Satan today? How does he feel about humans?

_____

_____

_____

Despite what many believe, Satan's headquarters for his rebellion is on the earth, not a place called "hell." In the book of Job, we learn that Satan walks to and fro upon the earth. In the Bible, where one's foot treads is often considered their domain. (See Deuteronomy 11:24; Joshua 1:3.)

Satan brought his terrible lies to Planet Earth. The apostle Peter says that Satan is like a lion seeking to devour humanity. Jesus called Satan the "ruler of this world" (John 12:31).

Battlefield Earth

Read: Genesis 1:26; 2:7–17; 3:1–13

React: What does it mean to be created in God's image? What did God say would be the result of eating from the tree of the knowledge of good and evil?

_____

_____

_____

Unlike the rest of the creation, God sculpted Adam and Eve with His own hands. He then placed them in a beautiful garden where they could enjoy their new paradise world in the same perfect harmony that the rest of heaven experienced.

However, God gave Adam and Eve a way to exercise their freewill by planting the tree of the knowledge of good and evil in the garden. By trusting God and not eating of the forbidden tree, they would have access to the tree of life forever. But if they embraced Satan's kingdom, they would cut themselves off from the source of life—God—and, naturally, would experience eternal death.

Read: Genesis 3:1–5; 1 John 2:16; James 1:15

React: What tactics did Satan use to convince Eve to eat from the forbidden tree? How has he tweaked his methods to convince humans to keep sinning?

_____

_____

_____

Satan used trickery and lies to deceive Eve. He took the form of a serpent, one of God's most beautiful and intelligent creations, to trick her into believing that God was not trustworthy. Through the serpent, Satan told Eve that not only would she become as wise as God by eating the fruit, but that God had also lied to her when He said that she would die.

As a result of acting on Satan's lies, Adam and Eve invited death and suffering into our world on an unimaginable scale—where even innocent children are murdered and abused for the selfish purposes of adults. It was Satan, not God, who brought heartache and pain to our planet.

Because Satan is the "father of lies" (John 8:44 NIV), he continues to use deception to make even the worst sins appear attractive to people today. Some of his most effective strategies have been to malign the character of God and to cast doubt on Scripture, because he knows that people will turn away from worshiping their Creator if they misunderstand Him and don't believe His Word.

Know Your Enemy

Because Satan has a profound effect on our world and in our lives today, it's important that we understand how he operates. That's why the Bible spends so much time revealing his character, especially in contrast to God's character.

Read: The Bible says that Satan ...

- Deceives and persecutes (Revelation 12:9, 13)
- Misuses Bible passages in order to trick people (Matthew 4:5, 6)
- Makes war against people who serve God (Revelation 12:10, 17)
- Traps and devours (2 Timothy 2:26; 1 Peter 5:8)
- Prompts people to betray one another (Luke 13:16; John 13:2, 21)
- Afflicts, murders, and brings sickness and disease (Job 2:7; John 8:44)
- Imprisons, possesses, and hinders (1 Thessalonians 2:18; Revelation 2:10; Luke 22:3–5)
- Appears as an angel of light; his demons can also impersonate the living and the dead (2 Corinthians 11:13–15)
- Can call fire down from heaven and perform other kinds of miracles (Revelation 13:13; Revelation 16:13, 14)

React: Knowing what the Bible says about Satan, are you better prepared to help those who are asking why there is so much evil in our world? Explain:

_____

_____

_____

Read: 1 Corinthians 13:4–8; 1 John 3:8

React: After reading the apostle Paul's chapter on the nature of love, do you understand better why God has allowed Satan, demons, and people to test the devil's principles here on earth? Why is it important to keep God's character in focus when we contemplate the battle between good and evil?

_____

_____

_____

Reflection and Discussion: Read Hebrews 2:14, Philippians 2:10, 11, and Nahum 1:9. How does it help you today, even as the devil continues his cruel work on earth, to know that God has already planned an end to the sin problem and has guaranteed that sin will not rise again in the new heavens and new earth?

_____

_____

_____

Your Questions Answered

Q. Isn't God responsible for sin because he created the devil?

A. God created Lucifer, a sinless angel. Lucifer made a devil of himself. Freedom to choose is a cornerstone principle of God's government, because without freewill, there cannot be genuine love. God knew that Lucifer would sin when He created him. If God had refused to create Lucifer, He would have been repudiating His own nature—which is selfless love. God is willing to be misunderstood and falsely accused while allowing every person to freely choose whom he or she will follow.

Q. Why didn't God destroy Lucifer and end the sin problem immediately?

A. Because sin was something new in God's creation and its inhabitants did not understand it. Lucifer's arguments convinced many angels, and a third joined him in rebellion. If God had destroyed Lucifer immediately, some angelic beings who did not fully understand God's character might have begun to obey God through fear rather than love. Nothing would have been settled in the minds of God's created beings if He had destroyed Lucifer immediately.

The Lord will abolish sin only after every soul in the universe is convinced of the truth—that Satan's government is unfair, hateful, ruthless, lying, and destructive. The Bible says, "We have been made a spectacle [theater] to the world, both to angels and to men" (1 Corinthians 4:9). The entire universe is watching as we each play a part in the controversy between Christ and Satan. As the controversy ends, every soul will fully understand the principles of both kingdoms and will have chosen to follow either Christ or Satan.

Firm Foundation

"Enemy-occupied territory—that is what this world is. Christianity is the story of how the rightful king has landed, you might say landed in disguise, and is calling us to take part in a great campaign of sabotage" (C.S. Lewis, *Mere Christianity*).

"The discord which his own course had caused in heaven, Satan charged upon the government of God. All evil he declared to be the result of the divine administration. He claimed that it was his own object to improve upon the statutes of Jehovah. Therefore God permitted him to demonstrate the nature of his claims, to show the working out of his proposed changes in the divine law. His own work must condemn him. Satan had claimed from the first that he was not in rebellion. The whole universe must see the deceiver unmasked. ... Even when he was cast out of heaven, Infinite Wisdom did not destroy Satan. Since only the service of love can be acceptable to God, the allegiance of His creatures must rest upon a conviction of His justice and benevolence. The inhabitants of heaven and of the worlds, being unprepared to comprehend the nature or consequences of sin, could not then have seen the justice of God in the destruction of Satan. Had he been immediately blotted out of existence, some would have served God from fear rather than from love. The influence of the deceiver would not have been fully destroyed, nor would the spirit of rebellion have been utterly eradicated. For the good of the entire universe through ceaseless ages, he must more fully develop his principles, that his charges against the divine government might be seen in their true light by all created beings, and that the justice and mercy of God and the immutability of His law might be forever placed beyond all question" (*Patriarchs and Prophets*, pp. 42, 43).

Lesson Summary

1. God created the universe based on the principles of selfless love and genuine freedom.

2. While Lucifer's role was to serve creation as a "light bearer" of God's love, he turned inward and sought to use his beauty and power to serve and exalt himself.

3. Now known as Satan, the devil seeks to destroy God's children on earth. He is the one who has brought death and destruction to our planet.

4. God is allowing the universe to see the fruit of Satan's lies and deception for a limited time, while promising to bring humanity salvation from sin and death.

Chapter Three
SALVATION, PART 2

The Gift of Life

Julie was only 27 years old when she discovered that she needed a kidney transplant. While her brother-in-law Stephen was a willing donor, he wasn't a match. So Julie entered into a "paired-donation" program, which enabled her to swap Stephen's kidney with the kidney of another willing donor.

However, when a match for Julie was finally found, she learned that her new kidney was from an unknown donor who was simply offering his kidney to her as a gift. "I don't think I'll ever get my head around it," Julie says. Quite literally, Julie received the gift of life—from a complete stranger.

After surgery, Julie says, "My life has completely changed." Her energy returned, her body doesn't ache, and she's free from dialysis. Best of all, she now has an infant daughter. "Because of that exceptional gift," she says, "we have our beautiful daughter and a future, and I will be forever grateful."

How might Julie's gratitude impact her future? Can you imagine her refusing to take anti-rejection medications or go to her regular doctor appointments? Of course not! Julie's gratitude for a better future will motivate her to take care of her kidney. "Every day, we're thankful," she says. "I don't think 'thank you' will ever be enough."

The gratitude didn't stop with Julie. Stephen donated his kidney anyway, even though it wasn't required to save Julie. "It was a huge mix of feelings knowing someone in my family was having such serious surgery for me," Julie says, "but he was so calm and focused." [1]

Christians have received a similar transplant. The gift of eternal life comes to us by grace alone. We can't earn it by who we are or what we do. But as with Julie and Stephen, the gift transforms our lives. We are new people, joyfully nurturing the gift we've been given and looking for ways to share it with others.

---

1   https://www.organdonationscotland.org/living-kidney-donation/donor-stories/julies-story

Hide Them in Your Heart

Memorize the following verses this week!

"For by grace you have been saved through faith, and that not of yourselves; it is the gift of God, not of works, lest anyone should boast. For we are His workmanship, created in Christ Jesus for good works, which God prepared beforehand that we should walk in them." —Ephesians 2:8–10

"Therefore, if anyone is in Christ, he is a new creation; old things have passed away; behold, all things have become new." —2 Corinthians 5:17

God's Agenda

Read: Ephesians 2:1–6

React: What were we like before God's salvation came into the picture?

_____

_____

_____

This passage is a beautiful summary of God's work of salvation. Despite everything we've done, the Lord did not idly allow our disobedience to take its natural course—death. He intervened!

Now there is a way of escape. We are made alive with Christ. Indeed, we are so closely aligned with Christ, living in Him, that His resurrection, ascension, and coronation also belong to us! This process is called justification. Through no merit of our own, a place has been secured for us in heaven. Just as though we'd never sinned, we are now exempt from the death sentence that sin brings.

Read: Ephesians 2:7

React: Why did God intervene in this marvelous way? (Look for the "so that.")

_____

_____

_____

Isn't it incredible? God's agenda—His reason for salvation—is so that He can show us kindness. He wants us to revel in the riches of His grace for eternity. Much like that altruistic kidney donor, God has given us a gift. It isn't about us—because, as we've seen, we're children of wrath, dead in our sins. Instead, it's about Him. _He_ is kind. _He_ is loving. _He_ is full of grace. And so, He gives.

But it doesn't end there! How could it? Such a gift must grow and get better all the time!

Reflection and Discussion: "For by grace you have been saved through faith, and that not of yourselves; it is the gift of God, not of works, lest anyone should boast" (Ephesians 2:8, 9). What does this verse mean to you in light of your life experience before you were saved?

_____

_____

_____

The Gift that Grows

Read: Philippians 1:3–11

React: What is the apostle Paul's desire for the Christians in Philippi?

_____

_____

_____

Paul asks for change and growth among believers. Note how such changes will be made: "by Jesus Christ." Jesus, having already given us righteousness through faith, next develops in us the fruit of righteousness. Bit by bit, Christ transforms us into His image: "We all, with unveiled face, beholding as in a mirror the glory of the Lord, are being transformed into the same image from glory to glory, just as by the Spirit of the Lord" (2 Corinthians 3:18). This process of gradual change is called sanctification—and Jesus is the one who started it and will finish it in us.

Read: Romans 8:10, 11; Acts 2:38; Luke 11:13

React: Who has the gift of the Holy Spirit?

_____

_____

_____

How does sanctification happen? Those who have accepted Christ's gift of justification are given another incredible gift—the Holy Spirit, who enables the sanctification process. The Holy Spirit gives at least two precious gifts for this purpose. First, the same power that resurrected Jesus is now available to us in order to "put to death the deeds of the body" (Romans 8:13). That's victory over sin!

Second, the Holy Spirit "bears witness with our spirit that we are children of God" (Romans 8:16). That's the assurance of salvation! Could there be any better gift?

Reflection and Discussion: How has your life changed since accepting Jesus' gift of salvation? What fruit of righteousness do you see Him developing in your life today?

_____

_____

_____

New Life

Read: Romans 6:1–14

React: What symbol does Paul use for death and rebirth?

_____

_____

_____

It seems some people in the early church wanted to take advantage of justification. *Oh, good—we get to go on sinning*, they thought. But Paul rejects that distortion: "Certainly not!" (Romans 6:2). Instead, the Christian will want to please the God they love.

Baptism is a powerful outward symbol of the transformation that has happened in the Christian's life. As they are buried beneath the water, they show they have died to sin. But as they are lifted out of the water, they show they have been resurrected to live a new kind of life.

After drawing the baptism parallel, Paul gives this instruction: "Likewise you also, reckon yourselves to be dead indeed to sin, but alive to God in Christ Jesus our Lord" (Romans 6:11). In the sanctification process, instead of letting sin have free reign, we give ourselves to God for righteousness. Let's find out what that looks like.

Read: Galatians 5:13–25

React: What does it look like to live by the Spirit?

_____

_____

_____

The contrast between the works of the flesh and the fruit of the Spirit highlights an important point: Living by the Spirit looks very similar to keeping the law! In fact, Paul says, "For all the law is fulfilled in one word, even in this: 'You shall love your neighbor as yourself.'"

The apostle John goes as far as to say: "For this is the love of God, that we keep His commandments. And His commandments are not burdensome" (1 John 5:3). The new life is freedom! Just as taking care of a new kidney would not be a burden, but a matter of joy and gratitude, so is the Christian life of maintaining obedience. After all, this life is not powered by determination, grit, or a long checklist; the Spirit-filled life is enabled by the resurrection power of God!

Glorious Expectation

Read: Titus 2:11–13; Philippians 3:20, 21; 1 Corinthians 15:51–57

React: As God sanctifies us, what can we look forward to?

_____

_____

_____

By faith in Christ, we are justified—saved from the *penalty* of our sins. By the Spirit, we are sanctified and saved from the *power* of sin in our lives.

Yet sweeter still is glorification, when we will be saved from the *presence* of sin. At the Second Coming, our mortal bodies will be changed into glorious and immortal bodies! What should our response to this truth be? "Therefore, my beloved brethren, be steadfast, immoveable, always abounding in the work of the Lord, knowing that your labor is not in vain in the Lord" (1 Corinthians 15:58).

Reflection and Discussion: Read Romans 8:16–25. How does the future glory compare with the present?

_____

_____

_____

Christian life on this sinful planet is not pain-free. We will suffer, but our suffering is not without purpose! Just as labor pains result in holding a newborn baby, the suffering of all creation has a glorious result. Like a child craning her neck to watch the road for her daddy's return, Christians are "eagerly waiting" for the "redemption of our body" (Romans 8:23). And this waiting is not just a matter of a few minutes: "We eagerly wait for it with perseverance" (Romans 8:25). But no matter how long it takes or how we groan while we wait, it will be worth it! When God's glory is at hand, our suffering will seem so light that it won't even be worth comparing.

Your Questions Answered

Q. What if I accept Jesus and His forgiveness but then I sin again?

A. "If we confess our sins, He is faithful and just to forgive us our sins and to cleanse us from all unrighteousness" (1 John 1:9). Let this promise reassure you: God always forgives the repentant sinner. John continues: "My little children, these things I write to you, so that you may not sin" (1 John 2:1). God wants us to have complete victory. In addition to forgiveness, God promises to cleanse us. He will keep working in our lives to give us that victory. While God's power is perfect and His promise complete, our own faith can falter. What then? John tells us: "If anyone sins, we have an Advocate with the Father, Jesus Christ the righteous" (1 John 2:1).

Are you struggling with sin? Jesus Christ is available to forgive, cleanse, and empower you to overcome. Keep your focus on Him—the more you see Him, the more you will be changed. "Beloved, now we are children of God; and it has not yet been revealed what we shall be, but we know that when He is revealed, we shall be like Him, for we shall see Him as He is" (1 John 3:2).

Q. Does being baptized mean that I'm not able to be tempted anymore?

A. No. The apostle Peter instructs us to "beware lest you also fall from your own steadfastness" (2 Peter 3:17). Even sanctified Christians must beware of temptation—and it wouldn't be temptation if it didn't entice you on some level. But there is good news! "The Lord knows how to deliver the godly out of temptations" (2 Peter 2:9).

Firm Foundation

"Since we are sinful, unholy, we cannot perfectly obey the holy law. We have no righteousness of our own with which to meet the claims of the law of God. But Christ has made a way of escape for us. He lived on earth amid trials and temptations such as we have to meet. He lived a sinless life. He died for us, and now He offers to take our sins and give us His righteousness. If you give yourself to Him, and accept Him as your Savior, then, sinful as your life may have been, for His sake you are accounted righteous. Christ's character stands in place of your character, and you are accepted before God just as if you had not sinned.

"More than this, Christ changes the heart. He abides in your heart by faith. You are to maintain this connection with Christ by faith and the continual surrender of your will to Him; and so long as you do this, He will work in you to will and to do according to His good pleasure. So you may say, 'The life which I now live in the flesh I live by the faith of the Son of God, who loved me, and gave Himself for me' (Galatians 2:20). So Jesus said to His disciples, 'It is not ye that speak, but the Spirit of your Father which speaketh in you' (Matthew 10:20). Then with Christ working in you, you will manifest the same spirit and do the same good works—works of righteousness, obedience" (Ellen White, *Steps to Christ*, p. 62).

Lesson Summary

1. Justification happens when we accept Jesus' death on the cross on our behalf. We are freed from the penalty of sin and given the Holy Spirit.

2. Sanctification is God's gradual work of changing us into His image.

3. The Holy Spirit's power is available and victory over sin is possible!

4. The new life, which includes keeping the commandments, is a joy and not a burden.

5. Jesus is our advocate when we sin. He forgives us and cleanses us.

6. Baptism is the outward symbol of the inward death to sin and new life in Christ.

7. Glorification is the final freedom from the presence of sin that happens at Christ's return.

Chapter Four
SACTUARY, PART 1

Divinity's Dwelling

Deep down in your heart, are you missing someone, yearning to see him or her again? It could be a parent, a spouse, a child, a sibling, or even a close friend.

Sometimes you can reach your loved one by phone, WhatsApp, Skype, or Facetime—allowing you to connect with them even though they are far away. But while it's nice to have this technology, it's not the same as being in their physical presence, is it? Something's missing.

The Bible reveals that God is going through the same thing. He is also yearning to have up-close, personal time with His children. God wants to manifest His unconditional love to you face-to-face.

However, there is a reason this isn't possible right now: sin. Our lawlessness has created a barrier, a wall, between us and the sublime presence of God. Not because sin harms God, but because it harms us; nothing impure can survive in the holy presence of the Creator.

The great news is that this separation isn't going to last forever. The Bible promises that in the new earth, the human family will dwell in God's presence again (Revelation 21:1–4). However, before this new paradise could become a reality, God created a special place here on earth where, despite the barrier of sin, He could dwell among His children. This place was called the earthly sanctuary, a building that God designed to show the world how He would solve the problem of sin so that humanity could once again dwell in His presence. This week, we'll explore this divine dwelling place.

Hide Them in Your Heart
Memorize the following verses this week!

"Let them make Me a sanctuary, that I may dwell among them." —Exodus 25:8

"Your way, O God, is in the sanctuary." —Psalm 77:13

The Original Plan

Read: Genesis 1:1–2:25

React: What was the purpose of everything that God created?

_____

_____

_____

During the creation story, we see the wonderful way in which God prepared this amazing planet for humans. We see His design, detail, and love in everything He made. This planet was a gift from God to humanity, and its purpose was for us to enjoy and rejoice in it while living in the presence of the Creator.

But God also planted a test of loyalty in the Garden of Eden: the tree of the knowledge of good and evil. The plan was for our first parents to confirm their loyalty to the Lord by obeying His commands. If this had happened, the earth would have remained under the jurisdiction of God's kingdom—but sadly, the Edenic world didn't last long.

Read: Genesis 3:1–24; Romans 6:16

React: What were the consequences of Adam and Eve's disobedience? What lessons can we learn?

_____

_____

_____

Adam and Eve followed the selfish desires of their hearts, leading them to disobey God—while also giving Satan dominion over their world. (See John 14:30.) Tragically, God's plan for an intimate, face-to-face relationship with humanity was shattered. Adam and Eve could no longer dwell in the presence of God since the virus of sin made it impossible for them. (See Isaiah 59:2; Romans 3:23, 5:12.)

However, God didn't remain idle in the face of the devil's victory. He responded with an amazing prophecy that revealed how He would solve the problem of sin.

Reflection and Discussion: Read Genesis 3:15, 21; 4:4. What did God say would happen to the devil? How did God manifest His mercy to fallen humanity?

_____

_____

_____

The Earthly Sanctuary

Immediately after the fall of our first parents, God began working to restore a personal relationship with humanity—from Adam to Noah to Abraham. But let's now fast forward to just after His liberation of the Israelites from Egypt, when He took those former slaves into the wilderness desert to reveal His plans of salvation in a stunning new way.

Read: Exodus 25:8, 9; 26:30; Hebrews 8:5

React: Why did God ask Moses to build a sanctuary? Where did Moses get the blueprint to build it?

_____

_____

_____

The Bible says that God wanted to have a place on earth where He could dwell among His children. The design for this tabernacle was given to Moses by God Himself—a model based on the temple in heaven. But there was even more that God wanted to accomplish through the sanctuary.

Read: 2 Samuel 7:1-13

React: What promise did God give King David regarding the sanctuary? Was there something more to the prophecy than his son Solomon? Explain:

_____

_____

_____

The purpose of the earthly sanctuary was to represent God's kingdom here on earth. The Creator promised David that through the king's "seed," He would establish an eternal kingdom that would never come to an end.

Read: Isaiah 9:6, 7; Galatians 3:16

React: Who is the "seed" in Bible prophecy? How can we know this?

_____

_____

_____

While the promised seed of David did include Solomon, it ultimately pointed to Jesus—the eternal King of Righteousness.

Reflection and Discussion: What is the primary message God is giving us through the sanctuary? Does this promise fill you with hope?

_____

_____

_____

The Daily Service in the Sanctuary

Knowing that God wanted to use the sanctuary as a dwelling place and as a revelation of how Jesus would restore righteousness in humanity, let's now look at its inner workings. The earthly sanctuary featured two primary services: the daily rituals and sacrifices and the yearly services and sacrifices, known as the Day of Atonement (Yom Kippur).

Read: Exodus 29:38–42; Leviticus 5:5, 6, 13; Numbers 28:1–8

React: What was offered on the altar as a sacrifice for sin? What did it mean?

_____

_____

_____

Read: John 1:29; 2 Corinthians 5:18–21; 1 Peter 1:18–21; Revelation 13:8

React: Who was represented by the animals sacrificed? What message was this meant to send fallen humanity?

_____

_____

_____

"The sacrificial offerings were ordained by God to be to man a perpetual reminder and a penitential acknowledgment of his sin and a confession of his faith in the promised Redeemer. They were intended to impress upon the fallen race the solemn truth that it was sin that caused death. To Adam, the offering of the first sacrifice was a most painful ceremony. ... As he slew the innocent victim, he trembled at the thought that his sin must shed the blood of the spotless Lamb of God. This scene gave him a deeper and more vivid sense of the greatness of his transgression, which nothing but the death of God's dear Son could expiate [atone for]. And he marveled at the infinite goodness that would give such a ransom to save the guilty. A star of hope illumined the dark and terrible future and relieved it of its utter desolation" (_Patriarchs and Prophets_, p. 30).

God's plan of salvation starts with the Lamb of God. That Jesus willingly left His throne in heaven to give us a chance to live in the presence of God again should give us an overwhelming sense of joy and admiration. (See John 3:16, 17; Philippians 2:5–8.)

Reflection and Discussion: What is your response to God in light of this awesome gift of love?

_____

_____

_____

The Furniture in the Sanctuary

The sanctuary structure was divided into three parts: the outer court, the Holy Place, and the Most Holy Place. Each part had specific pieces of furniture within designed to reveal something about God's plan of salvation.

As you read, ask yourself two questions. What is the purpose of each piece of furniture in the earthly sanctuary? What does each piece of furniture represent prophetically in the New Covenant?

Outer Court | Altar of Sacrifice: Leviticus 1:1–5; Luke 23:33, 34

_____

_____

_____

Outer Court | Laver: Exodus 30:17–21; Romans 6:4, 5

_____

_____

_____

Holy Place | Table of Shewbread: Leviticus 24:5–9; Luke 4:1–4

_____

_____

_____

Holy Place | Candlestick: Leviticus 24:1–4; Zechariah 4:1–6; Revelation 1:20, 4:5

_____

_____

_____

Holy Place | Altar of Incense: Exodus 30:1–8; Revelation 8:3, 4

_____

_____

_____

Holy Place | Veil: Exodus 26:31–33; Hebrews 10:19, 20

_____

_____

_____

Most Holy Place | Ark of the Covenant: Exodus 25:10–22; Deuteronomy 10:1–5; Isaiah 6:1–3

_____

_____

_____

In vision, the apostle John was granted a view of God's temple in heaven, seeing "seven lamps of fire were burning before the throne" (Revelation 4:5) and "a golden censer" with "incense" (Revelation 8:3). Both these items are seen in the Holy Place on earth: the golden candlestick and the altar of incense. John also saw the ark of the covenant, in which the Ten Commandment tablets were placed.

"In the temple in heaven, the dwelling place of God, His throne is established in righteousness and judgment. In the most holy place is His law, the great rule of right by which all mankind are tested. The ark that enshrines the tables of the law is covered with the mercy seat, before which Christ pleads His blood in the sinner's behalf. Thus is represented the union of justice and mercy in the plan of human redemption. This union infinite wisdom alone could devise and infinite power accomplish; it is a union that fills all heaven with wonder and adoration. The cherubim of the earthly sanctuary, looking reverently down upon the mercy seat, represent the interest with which the heavenly host contemplate the work of redemption. This is the mystery of mercy into which angels desire to look—that God can be just while He justifies the repenting sinner and renews His intercourse with the fallen race; that Christ could stoop to raise unnumbered multitudes from the abyss of ruin and clothe them with the spotless garments of His own righteousness to unite with angels who have never fallen and to dwell forever in the presence of God" (_The Great Controversy_, p. 415).

Feast Days in the Sanctuary

Let's now turn to the Hebrew religious calendar, which had seven feast days associated with God's plan of salvation. (See Leviticus 23:1, 2.) As with the furniture, these feast days had a deeper reality: prophecies that pointed to Jesus' work in the heavenly sanctuary. As you read, ask yourself: What stands out in each of the feast days? How is Christ's ministry associated with each one?

Passover: Leviticus 23:5; 1 Corinthians 5:7

_____

_____

Unleavened Bread: Leviticus 23:6; 1 Corinthians 5:7, 8; Acts 13:35–37

_____

_____

First Fruits: Leviticus 23:10, 11; 1 Corinthians 15:20–23

_____

_____

Weeks/Pentecost: Leviticus 23:15, 16; Acts 2:1–47

_____

_____

Trumpets: Leviticus 23:24; Revelation 8:2, 6

_____

_____

Tabernacles/Booths: Leviticus 23:34; Revelation 21:3, 4

_____

_____

Day of Atonement: We will focus on this feast in detail next week.

"The matchless splendor of the earthly tabernacle reflected to human vision the glories of that heavenly temple where Christ our forerunner ministers for us before the throne of God. The abiding place of the King of kings, where thousand thousands minister unto Him, and ten thousand times ten thousand stand before Him (Daniel 7:10); that temple, filled with the glory of the eternal throne, where seraphim, its shining guardians, veil their faces in adoration, could find, in the most magnificent structure ever reared by human hands, but a faint reflection of its vastness and glory. Yet important truths concerning the heavenly sanctuary and the great work there carried forward for man's redemption, were taught by the earthly sanctuary and its services" (*The Great Controversy*, p. 414).

Firm Foundation

"The sanctuary in heaven is the very center of Christ's work in behalf of men. It concerns every soul living upon the earth. It opens to view the plan of redemption, bringing us down to the very close of time, and revealing the triumphant issue of the contest between righteousness and sin. It is of the utmost importance that all should thoroughly investigate these subjects, and be able to give an answer to every one that asketh them a reason of the hope that is in them.

"The intercession of Christ in man's behalf in the sanctuary above is as essential to the plan of salvation as was His death upon the cross. By His death He began that work which after His resurrection He ascended to complete in heaven. We must by faith enter within the veil, 'whither the forerunner is for us entered' (Hebrews 6:20). There the light from the cross of Calvary is reflected. There we may gain a clearer insight into the mysteries of redemption. The salvation of man is accomplished at an infinite expense to heaven; the sacrifice made is equal to the broadest demands of the broken law of God. Jesus has opened the way to the Father's throne, and through His mediation the sincere desire of all who come to Him in faith may be presented before God" (*The Great Controversy*, pp. 488, 489).

"Those who were studying the subject found indisputable proof of the existence of a sanctuary in heaven. Moses made the earthly sanctuary after a pattern which was shown him. Paul teaches that that pattern was the true sanctuary which is in heaven. And John testifies that he saw it in heaven" (*The Great Controversy*, p. 415).

Lesson Summary

1. God desires to have face-to-face communion with humanity again.

2. Sin caused division between humanity and divinity, but Jesus Christ, through His sacrifice on the cross, opened the door for us to be restored in our relationship with the Creator.

3. Through the sanctuary, God details the process through which He will separate us from our sin.

4. The real plan of salvation is being carried out in the heavenly sanctuary and is being ministered by Jesus as our Lamb, High Priest, and King.

Chapter Five
SACTUARY PART 2

Heaven's Court

Have you ever felt like you were being watched by someone you couldn't see? It can be quite a creepy feeling!

Well, did you know that the Bible says everything you do here on earth is being analyzed and scrutinized down to the last detail? Would that change how you live your life? "God will bring every work into judgment, including every secret thing, whether good or evil" (Ecclesiastes 12:14). This can be a dreadful thought when you realize how many times you've "sinned and fallen short of the glory of God."

However, there is good news! "My little children, these things I write to you, so that you may not sin. And if anyone sins, we have an Advocate with the Father, Jesus Christ the righteous" (1 John 2:1). Despite our shortcomings, we can have assurance that Christ is advocating for us in heaven's court.

Last week, we looked at six of the feast days associated with the sanctuary services; this week, we'll look at the Day of Atonement (also known as Yom Kippur), which will help you better understand the work of Christ as our Intercessor in the heavenly sanctuary and the wonderful truth about the end of sin.

Hide Them in Your Heart
Memorize the following verses this week!

"I saw another angel flying in the midst of heaven, having the everlasting gospel to preach to those who dwell on the earth—to every nation, tribe, tongue, and people—saying with a loud voice, 'Fear God and give glory to Him, for the hour of His judgment has come; and worship Him who made heaven and earth, the sea and springs of water.'" —Revelation 14:6, 7

"He said to me, 'For two thousand three hundred days; then the sanctuary shall be cleansed.'" —Daniel 8:14

Why a Judgment?

Many look at our world today and wonder: "Why is there so much pain? Why do good people suffer? Why doesn't God do something about it now?" These are reasonable questions we've all asked at some point in our lives. In the Bible, we even find many people of faith asking these same questions.

Read: Psalm 73:1–14

React: How should believers respond to someone concerned about the injustices experienced so often in our world?

_____

_____

_____

Why does it seem that God allows the unrepentant to experience the good life while believers often struggle? It doesn't seem fair, does it? Psalm 73 even presents one believer having serious doubts about serving God because he feels he has nothing to show for his obedience.

Read: Psalm 73:15–19

React: What changed in the writer's perception of reality from the previous verses?

_____

_____

_____

The sanctuary changed everything! The psalmist became aware that the unjust conditions of the world would one day change and that justice would be ultimately restored. In this picture of the temple, he saw God's judgment being carried out through its many services, sacrifices, and feast days—all leading to a vindication of God's will and character. Through the sanctuary, we can also learn to trust in God's love and in His plan to end the great controversy being waged here on planet Earth.

Reflection and Discussion: What are some ways you can share your trust in and love of God's promises with others who might doubt His character because of the pain and suffering they are experiencing?

_____

_____

_____

The Yearly Cleansing

Throughout the Hebrew religious year, many sins were taken into the sanctuary by the ministration of the blood of sacrificed animals. On the Day of Atonement, also known as the day of judgment, this defilement was addressed. Let's look at the symbols and the greater truths to which they pointed.

Read: Leviticus 16:7–11, 15; Hebrews 9:11–14, 22; Revelation 20:1–3

React: What happened to each goat? Who does each goat represent?

_____

_____

_____

Read: Leviticus 16:16; Daniel 8:14

React: What was cleansed on the Day of Atonement? Why was it necessary?

_____

_____

_____

"The blood of Christ, while it was to release the repentant sinner from the condemnation of the law, was not to cancel the sin; it would stand on record in the sanctuary until the final atonement; so in the type the blood of the sin offering removed the sin from the penitent, but it rested in the sanctuary until the Day of Atonement" (*Patriarchs and Prophets*, p. 357).

All the confessed sins of the Israelites during the year remained in the sanctuary. The purpose of the Day of Atonement was to remove these sins through the two goats so that God could continue dwelling with His people. Christ was represented by the goat sacrificed, cleansing us from sin (Hebrews 9:22). Satan was the scapegoat led off into the wilderness; it was on the scapegoat's head that all the sins were transferred, showing that Satan bears the ultimate responsibility in leading the rebellion that has caused so much suffering here on the earth.

Read: Leviticus 16:32–34; Hebrews 8:1–6

React: What was the role of the high priest on the Day of Atonement? How does Jesus fulfill this role for humanity?

_____

_____

_____

The high priest's role was to mediate between God and His children, entering into the Most Holy Place only once per year. This day of judgment was a call for the people of Israel to repent from their sinful deeds in gratitude for God's forgiveness.

Reflection and Discussion: How can Hebrews 4:14–16 give you hope and joy in the day of judgment to come, rather than fear?

_____

_____

_____

Atonement in the New Covenant, Part 1

Now that we have a basic understanding of the Day of Atonement, let's look closely at its prophetic fulfillment, the great judgment day in the heavenly court.

Read: Revelation 14:6, 7; 22:12

React: What do we learn about God's judgment? What is Christ bringing with Him when He returns?

_____

_____

_____

The apostle John's vision concerning the end-times reveals that God's judgment has already begun. This is surprising to Christians who have been taught that the judgment won't occur until after Christ returns. Yet Jesus is coming with rewards—which means a judgment about who gets those rewards has already been made! So when did this judgment begin?

Read: Daniel 7:9, 10

React: What event is happening—and where is it taking place?

_____

_____

_____

The prophet Daniel saw a judgment happening before the throne of God, which is in the heavenly sanctuary.

"The matchless splendor of the earthly tabernacle reflected to human vision the glories of that heavenly temple where Christ our forerunner ministers for us before the throne of God. The abiding place of the King of kings, where thousand thousands minister unto Him, and ten thousand times ten thousand stand before Him (Daniel 7:10); that temple, filled with the glory of the eternal throne, where seraphim, its shining guardians, veil their faces in adoration, could find, in the most magnificent structure ever reared by human hands, but a faint reflection of its vastness and glory. Yet important truths concerning the heavenly sanctuary and the great work there carried forward for man's redemption were taught by the earthly sanctuary and its services" (*The Great Controversy*, p. 414).

Atonement in the New Covenant, Part 2

The book of Daniel chapter 8 shares another extraordinary vision that will help us better understand the judgment.

Read: Daniel 8:9–14

React: Where is this event taking place and who is described? Where have we seen this before and what sanctuary is being mentioned?

_____

_____

_____

Here we are presented with a scene in which a little horn power (Daniel 7:8, 24, 25) is trampling on the sanctuary, attempting to dominate heaven and earth, disrupt God's plan of salvation, and take God's place on His throne (2 Thessalonians 2:3, 4). However, despite this antichrist power's best efforts, God will cleanse His sanctuary from its influence. This cleansing takes place after the judgment in Daniel chapter 7. Let's now look a little closer.

Read: Numbers 14:34; Ezekiel 4:6; Luke 13:32

React: What prophetic principle is revealed in these verses? How does it help us understand when the great day of judgment would begin?

_____

_____

_____

In apocalyptic literature, a prophetic day equates to a literal year of time. Thus, the actual time of the 2,300 days in Daniel 8:14 is really 2,300 years—revealing the longest time prophecy in the Bible! But when did this prophecy begin?

Read: Daniel 9:20–25

React: What is the connection to the 2,300 days in Daniel 8:14 and 9:23, 24? What clue helps us find the starting date for the prophecy?

_____

_____

_____

"The 2300 days had been found to begin when the commandment of Artaxerxes for the restoration and building of Jerusalem went into effect, in the autumn of 457 BC. Taking this as the starting point, there was perfect harmony in the application of all the events foretold in the explanation of that period in Daniel 9:25–27. Sixty-nine weeks, the first 483 of the 2300 years, were to reach to the Messiah, the Anointed One; and Christ's baptism and anointing by the Holy Spirit, AD 27, exactly fulfilled the specification. In the midst of the seventieth week, Messiah was to be cut off. Three and a half years after His baptism, Christ was crucified, in the spring of AD 31. The seventy weeks, or 490 years, were to pertain especially to the Jews. At the expiration of this period the nation sealed its rejection of Christ by the persecution of His disciples, and the apostles turned to the Gentiles, AD 34. The first 490 years of the 2300 having then ended, 1810 years would remain. From AD 34, 1810 years extend to 1844. 'Then,' said the angel, 'shall the sanctuary be cleansed.' All the preceding specifications of the prophecy had been unquestionably fulfilled at the time appointed. With this reckoning, all was clear and harmonious, except that it was not seen that any event answering to the cleansing of the sanctuary had taken place in 1844. To deny that the days ended at that time was to involve the whole question in confusion, and to renounce positions which had been established by unmistakable fulfillments of prophecy" (*The Great Controversy*, p. 410).

Jesus began His High Priest ministry in the heavenly sanctuary in the autumn of 1844. We now have the assurance that He represents everyone who comes to Him, faithfully presenting our case before the Father in the heavenly court.

Your Questions Answered

Q. If the dead "sleep," how can they attend their court hearing in heaven?

A. No man could enter into the Most Holy Place except the high priest (Leviticus 16:17). Likewise, only the sinless Christ is able to stand in the presence of God the Father in the judgment. The good news is that He is there to serve as our Advocate (1 John 2:1). "Christ has not entered the holy places made with hands ... but into heaven itself, now to appear in the presence of God for us" (Hebrews 9:24).

Q. Don't only the lost experience judgment since there is no condemnation for those who are in Christ?

A. The Bible says, "We must all appear before the judgment seat of Christ, that each one may receive the things done ... whether good or bad" (2 Corinthians 5:10). See also Romans 14:12. However, while the judgment condemns the unrepentant, it vindicates God's people (Revelation 12:10).

Q. Why is it that most Christians aren't aware of the sanctuary as revealing God's full plan of salvation nor its significance in prophecy?

A. The devil doesn't want anyone to be saved, so he is using the little horn power and the beast to attack the sanctuary message (Daniel 8:9–12; Revelation 13:2, 6), changing our focus with deceptions. He knows that if he can keep Christians away from understanding the full plan of salvation, he has a better chance to keep them enslaved to sin and unaware of the great promises God has in store for them. Praise the Lord we have Christ ministering for us in heaven, His Holy Spirit ministering here on earth, and His Word to guide us to both!

Firm Foundation

"The subject of the sanctuary and the investigative judgment should be clearly understood by the people of God. All need a knowledge for themselves of the position and work of their great High Priest. Otherwise it will be impossible for them to exercise the faith which is essential at this time or to occupy the position which God designs them to fill" (*The Great Controversy*, p. 488).

"The work of the investigative judgment and the blotting out of sins is to be accomplished before the second advent of the Lord. Since the dead are to be judged out of the things written in the books, it is impossible that the sins of men should be blotted out until after the judgment at which their cases are to be investigated. But the apostle Peter distinctly states that the sins of believers will be blotted out, 'when the times of refreshing shall come from the presence of the Lord; and he shall send Jesus Christ' (Acts 3:19, 20). When the investigative judgment closes, Christ will come, and His reward will be with Him to give to every man as his work shall be.

"In the typical service the high priest, having made the atonement for Israel, came forth and blessed the congregation. So Christ, at the close of his work as a mediator, will appear, 'without sin unto salvation' (Hebrews 9:28), to bless His waiting people with eternal life. As the priest, in removing the sins from the sanctuary, confessed them upon the head of the scapegoat, so Christ will place all these sins upon Satan, the originator and instigator of sin. The scapegoat, bearing the sins of Israel, was sent away 'unto a land not inhabited" (Leviticus 16:22); so Satan, bearing the guilt of all the sins which he has caused God's people to commit, will be for a thousand years confined to the earth, which will then be desolate, without inhabitant, and he will at last suffer the full penalty of sin in the fires that shall destroy all the wicked. Thus the great plan of redemption will reach its accomplishment in the final eradication of sin and the deliverance of all who have been willing to renounce evil" (*The Great Controversy*, pp. 485, 486).

Lesson Summary

1. The Day of Atonement was a symbol of the real judgment in heaven, where Jesus serves as our Advocate and High Priest.

2. The judgment is being carried out in the heavenly sanctuary, where our works are presented as evidence of our profession of faith in Jesus Christ.

3. Based on the time prophecies of Daniel 8:14 and 9:23–25, we can know that judgment began in the autumn of 1844.

4. The purpose of the judgment isn't to condemn the faithful, but to vindicate God's character in deciding who is saved and who is lost.

5. After this judgment is complete, Christ will leave the heavenly sanctuary and come to save His people from all the ages.

Chapter Six
STATE OF MAN IN DEATH, PART 1

Exploring the Grave

Distraught after the deaths of her infant daughter and her husband, Sarah Winchester uprooted, moved west to San Jose, California, and purchased an eight-room house. From 1886 to 1922, Sarah's workers labored nonstop to transform her home into an extensive mansion. At just over 24,000 square feet, it contained 10,000 windows, 2,000 doors, 160 rooms, 13 bathrooms, and 6 kitchens.[1]

What drove the extremely wealthy socialite to isolate herself from society and dedicate the remaining 36 years of her life to such a sprawling construction project? Sarah, the heiress of the Winchester gunmaker fortune, appears to have suffered from guilt and a fear of the curse of the "spirits" of people who had passed as victims of the Winchester rifle. She believed it was the spirits who instructed her, through séances, to continue building in order to appease the angry dead. Mysteriously designed, many doors open to walls and stairways end at ceilings—as the spirits seemingly directed.[2]

The growing guest list of more than 12 million visitors at the Winchester home museum speaks to society's interest in the supernatural today. As Benjamin Franklin humorously stated, "In this world, nothing can be said to be certain, except death and taxes." With the guarantee of death before us, there are questions we all ask: What happens the moment after death? Heaven? Hell? Nothing?

Today, we begin a journey of exploring the biblical answer to life after death—an answer of hope and freedom that can truly "release those who through fear of death were all their lifetime subject to bondage" (Hebrews 2:15).

---

1   https://winchestermysteryhouse.com/sarahs-story/
2   https://www.biography.com/people/sarah-winchester

Hide Them in Your Heart

Memorize the following verses this week!

"Do not marvel at this; for the hour is coming in which all who are in the graves will hear His voice and come forth—those who have done good, to the resurrection of life, and those who have done evil, to the resurrection of condemnation." —John 5:28, 29

"Behold, I tell you a mystery: We shall not all sleep, but we shall all be changed—in a moment, in the twinkling of an eye, at the last trumpet. For the trumpet will sound, and the dead will be raised incorruptible, and we shall be changed. For this corruptible must put on incorruption, and this mortal must put on immortality." —1 Corinthians 15:51–53

The First Lie

Read: Genesis 3:1–4, 22–24

React: What lie did Satan tell Eve? After Adam and Eve sinned, why did God block them from eating from the tree of life?

_____

_____

_____

Though the heart of God yearned to continue dwelling with Adam and Eve in their garden home, He knew the stakes were too high. If they would keep eating from the tree of life, they would become eternal sinners. Thus, God sent an angel to block them from the tree, preventing humankind from the curse of immortality in their sinful state.

Read: Ezekiel 18:4; 1 Timothy 6:15, 16; 1 Corinthians 15:51–53

React: But doesn't the Bible say we have an immortal soul?

_____

_____

_____

The Bible uses the word "soul" approximately 1,600 times, but never once does it use the expression "immortal soul." Rather, it plainly states that the soul that sins will die. Romans 3:23 emphasizes that we all have sinned; thus, are all deserving of death. According to the Bible, only God has immortality—we are naturally mortal. The gift of immortality will be given to the redeemed at the second coming of Christ, when the dead in Christ are raised to eternal life.

Read: Genesis 2:7; Ecclesiastes 12:7

React: What then is a soul?

_____

_____

_____

To answer this question, we must look back to the creation story. God created man out of the dust of the earth and breathed into his nostrils the breath of life. We could say that man was created from two elements: dust and air. When breath is removed from the nostrils of man, he simply goes back (ultimately) to dust.

The Moment After Life

"Jesus, where were you? If you had been here, my brother wouldn't have died!" As their loved ones have tragically passed away, Martha, Mary, and countless billions have asked questions like this one through the centuries.

But in their moment of great tragedy, Jesus offered hope.

Read: John 11:11–14; Matthew 27:52; 1 Thessalonians 4:14

React: What did Jesus compare death to?

_____

_____

_____

Have you ever put your head on a pillow just to "rest your eyes" for a minute or two and, suddenly, two hours later, you're awake and wondering how it all sped by so quickly? Jesus compares death to a similar sleep.

And according to the Bible, when our loved ones pass away, their pain, their worries, and their fears all cease to exist. They are "sleeping" until Resurrection Day, when Jesus calls them and us home!

Read: Ecclesiastes 9:5–10; Psalm 115:17; Psalm 146:4; John 5:28, 29; Acts 2:29, 34

React: Is there awareness in the grave? Do the spirits of the dead return to haunt the living?

_____

_____

_____

According to the Bible, the dead are not in heaven. This includes the patriarch David. Instead, the dead are sleeping a dreamless, peaceful sleep until the coming of Jesus Christ.

Reflection and Discussion: Why does this knowledge of death bring more comfort and hope than believing that your loved one is in heaven looking down on you?

_____

_____

_____

57

Spiritualism's Deadly Trap

Read: 2 Corinthians 11:14; 1 Timothy 4:1

React: What is the danger of believing that the soul is immortal?

_____

_____

_____

Believing that we have immortal souls opens the door to spiritualism. The Bible warns that the devil can appear as an angel of light, and he certainly can impersonate our deceased loved ones. This is why, even while something may appear to be a beautiful message sent from God, we must faithfully test it by Scripture to confirm whether or not it is true. Ultimately, we cannot trust our emotions or even our eyes, but we can fully trust the Word of God.

Read: Matthew 24:23, 24; Revelation 13:13, 14; Revelation 16:14

React: Do devils really work miracles? Why is this knowledge of death such a crucial end-time message?

_____

_____

_____

Jesus warned that false prophets will work great wonders on earth. But no matter how miraculous someone's feats of power may seem, it doesn't mean they were sent from God.

Most of the people in the world will believe that through these false signs, Christ himself and His angels are leading out in a fantastic worldwide revival. The emphasis will seem so spiritual and be so overwhelming that only God's elect will not be deceived.

This is why God warns His last-day people that we must not have anything to do with spiritualism, not even allowing our curiosity or misplaced self-confidence to bring us close (Matthew 24:24–26; Deuteronomy 18:9–12; Leviticus 19:31). The apostle Paul warns, "But even if we, or an angel from heaven, preach any other gospel to you than what we have preached to you, let him be accursed" (Galatians 1:8). As noble Bereans, we must compare everything, even supposed messages or signs from heaven, back to the Bible as our only source of security—and the antidote against deception (Acts 17:10, 11; Isaiah 8:20).

A Fearless Death

"Baby, don't die," the desperate father cried out. "Please keep breathing. Don't die on me!" He tearfully pled for her life, but it was to no avail. His daughter gasped for her last breath of air. "Oh, God! No!" The father's anguish pierced the darkness of night.

False teachings had silently crept their way into the early church. The fledgling Thessalonian flock was persuaded that unless their loved ones were alive at the coming of Christ, they would never see them again. (See *The Acts of the Apostles*, p. 258). With no hope of a resurrection in their hearts, they were crushed with overwhelming despair—as one by one, their loved ones died and were delivered into the darkness of a supposedly eternal grave.

Yet their cries of agony had not passed unheard by their Father in heaven. With trembling hands, they grasped a weatherworn letter penned by the hand of a humble servant of God.

Read: 1 Thessalonians 4:16–18

React: What promise did Paul provide about the resurrection? When will it occur?

_____

_____

_____

There was hope! The death of their loved ones would not be eternal. Indeed, Death's grasp cannot restrain its victims when the shout of the Lifegiver sounds! Peace flooded the aching souls of the Thessalonian Christians.

Though centuries have passed since this message of hope was first received, how often we live our lives with the same overwhelming fear, as though this earth is our final resting place. While grasping in futility for this mortal life, eternal realities slip through our fingers.

God is calling us to look beyond the grave—for there stands Jesus! In their resurrected glory, His children will reunite with their loved ones. No trace of death or pain will be seen on the faces reflecting their Father's love. We'll spend an eternity basking in the presence of Him whose love sets us free! Truly, we can "comfort one another with these words."

Read: 1 Corinthians 15:26

React: For thousands of years, sin and death have wreaked havoc upon the earth, leaving no one outside the pain of their grasp. When will this curse finally end?

_____

_____

_____

The last enemy to be destroyed is death itself. Revelation 21:4 promises there will come a day when "God will wipe away every tear from their eyes; there shall be no more death, nor sorrow, nor crying. There shall be no more pain, for the former things have passed away."

Your Questions Answered

Q. Doesn't the apostle Paul say, "Absent from the body is to be present with the Lord"? (See 2 Corinthians 5:6–8.)

A. Note that verse 6 begins with the word "so"—or "therefore" in the King James. This indicates that what Paul is about to say is based on the hope of the Second Coming that he had just described in the previous verses. Beginning in 2 Corinthians 4:16–18, Paul was encouraging the Corinthian believers to not fear persecution and death. In 2 Corinthians 5:1, he contrasts our earthly bodies with our future glorified, heavenly bodies. In verse 4, he assures the believers that we will be clothed with our heavenly bodies when "that mortality may be swallowed up by life."

The question is: When does this occur? 1 Corinthians 15:51–54 holds the key. The language used is reminiscent of Paul's language in 2 Corinthians 5:1–4, where he speaks of being "clothed" with our heavenly bodies (i.e., immortality) and of death being "swallowed up" by life (1 Corinthians 15: 53, 54). In both 2 Corinthians 5 and 1 Corinthians 15, Paul is longing for the immortality that will be bestowed upon Jesus' return, and he is using this promise to encourage the Corinthians to not lose hope in the face of persecution that may result in death. If we are "absent" from our bodies, we would "be at home with the Lord," because our next conscious thought would be the resurrection and the sight of Jesus coming in the clouds. In this sense, Paul makes the case that death is preferable.

Q. What does Revelation 6:9–11 mean when it describes the souls under the altar crying with a loud voice?

A. To understand this passage, we must start at the beginning. In Genesis 4:10, when God confronts Cain for the slaying of his brother, He inquires, "What have you done? The voice of your brother's blood cries out to Me from the ground." In this passage, Abel's blood is described as crying out, but obviously, it was not meant to be taken literally. Rather, the Bible is using personification to drive home another point. This theme is repeated in Hebrews 12:24, when Jesus' blood is described as speaking "better things than that of Abel." This cannot be taken literally either. Likewise, Revelation is a book filled with symbols, so we need to carefully discern between the literal and the symbolic as we read through it.

When seeking to understand any Bible text, it is crucial to utilize the "fencepost method" of biblical interpretation. If you have a long line of ninety-nine perfectly symmetrical fence posts but notice one far out of place, would you adjust the ninety-nine or would you adjust the one? Similarly, if there is an apparent discrepancy between verses, instead of uprooting the many clear texts to make them fit a few tricky texts, interpret the few texts in light of the many.

Using this method, Hebrews 11:4 provides the key for understanding Revelation 6:9–11 when it speaks of Abel's death: "Through it he being dead still speaks." It is our memory of his righteousness that still speaks to us today. Similarly, it is the righteous character of the martyrs that still speaks from under the altar though they are dead. God remembers their sacrifices and their humble devotion to Him.

The context of both passages is the sacrifice that they made. And God forgets neither Abel nor these martyrs. Psalm 116:15 reminds us, "Precious in the sight of the Lord is the death of His saints." And in John 11:35, we see that Jesus even wept over the death of His friend Lazarus, showing that He understood and cared about human sorrow. We can be thankful that God promises, one day soon He'll raise His slain children back to life!

Firm Foundation

"The doctrine of man's consciousness in death, especially the belief that spirits of the dead return to minister to the living, has prepared the way for modern spiritualism. If the dead are admitted to the presence of God and holy angels, and privileged with knowledge far exceeding what they before possessed, why should they not return to the earth to enlighten and instruct the living? If, as taught by popular theologians, spirits of the dead are hovering about their friends on earth, why should they not be permitted to communicate with them, to warn them against evil, or to comfort them in sorrow? How can those who believe in man's consciousness in death reject what comes to them as divine light communicated by glorified spirits? Here is a channel regarded as sacred, through which Satan works for the accomplishment of his purposes. The fallen angels who do his bidding appear as messengers from the spirit world. While professing to bring the living into communication with the dead, the prince of evil exercises his bewitching influence upon their minds" (*The Great Controversy*, p. 551).

"He has power to bring before men the appearance of their departed friends. The counterfeit is perfect; the familiar look, the words, the tone, are reproduced with marvelous distinctness. Many are comforted with the assurance that their loved ones are enjoying the bliss of heaven, and without suspicion of danger, they give ear 'to seducing spirits, and doctrines of devils.' ...Then, as confidence is gained, they present doctrines that directly undermine faith in the Scriptures. With an appearance of deep interest in the well-being of their friends on earth, they insinuate the most dangerous errors. The fact that they state some truths, and are able at times to foretell future events, gives to their statements an appearance of reliability; and their false teachings are accepted by the multitudes as readily, and believed as implicitly, as if they were the most sacred truths of the Bible. The law of God is set aside, the Spirit of grace despised, the blood of the covenant counted an unholy thing" (ibid., p. 552).

"None need be deceived by the lying claims of spiritualism. God has given the world sufficient light to enable them to discover the snare. As already shown, the theory which forms the very foundation of spiritualism is at war with the plainest statements of Scripture. The Bible declares that the dead know not anything, that their thoughts have perished; they have no part in anything that is done under the sun; they know nothing of the joys or sorrows of those who were dearest to them on earth" (ibid., p. 556).

Lesson Summary

1. God alone has immortality; the saved will be given this gift at the resurrection.

2. We can have comfort knowing that our loved ones are sleeping peacefully until the second coming of Christ.

3. There is no need to fear death when we trust in the Author of Life!

Chapter Seven
STATE OF MAN IN DEATH, PART 2

Questioning Hellfire

Jonathan Edwards, the famous revivalist of the mid-eighteenth century, left a lasting impact on countless souls with his most widely known sermon: "Sinners in the Hands of an Angry God."

While the congregation sat in hushed silence, Edwards preached, "The God that holds you over the pit of hell, much as one holds a spider, or some loathsome insect, over the fire, abhors you and is dreadfully provoked; his wrath toward you burns like fire; he looks upon you as worthy of nothing else!"

This chilling description was then concluded with the appeal, "Therefore, let everyone that is out of Christ now awake and fly from the wrath to come." With moans of grief and tears of repentance, many who had gathered naturally made the desired decision. But did it last?

Many biblical scholars today are questioning the doctrine of an eternally burning hell, seeing it as contradictory to the loving character of God. Yet others claim that removing the fear of hell will cause many to walk away from Christianity and to live immoral lives.

But what does the Bible say? Is there an eternally burning hell or not? This week, we'll discover that the clear answer about hell offers hope for us today.

Hide Them in Your Heart
Memorize the following verses this week!

"'As I live,' says the Lord God, 'I have no pleasure in the death of the wicked, but that the wicked turn from his way and live. Turn, turn from your evil ways! For why should you die, O house of Israel?'" —Ezekiel 33:11

"For the Son of Man did not come to destroy men's lives but to save them." —Luke 9:56

"For the wages of sin is death, but the gift of God is eternal life in Christ Jesus our Lord." —Romans 6:23

In Search of Hell

The term "hell" occurs 54 times in the King James Bible. (Newer translations use the words "Hades" and "Sheol" instead, so there are fewer occurrences of the word "hell.") Of these 54 occurrences, 41 of them are in reference to "the grave" or, at the very least, not a place of burning. In the New Testament, just 12 usages of the word "hell" refers to "Gehenna," which is a place of burning.

There are three important questions to answer about hell: When will it burn? Where will it burn? And how long will it burn? Let's look at the Bible's answers.

Read: Matthew 13:24–30, 37–40; 2 Peter 2:4, 9; Job 21:30

React: When will hell fire burn?

_____

_____

_____

According to these verses, the wicked are being "reserved" for judgment—that means at a time later than when the passage was being written.

Read: John 5:28, 29

React: When will this judgment take place?

_____

_____

_____

If the wicked were sent to hell the moment they died, as many believe, they would be receiving their judgment *before* the resurrection. But according to the Bible, the judgment—for either life or damnation—is delivered *at* the resurrection.

Reflection and Discussion: Does it really matter what you believe about hell? How could a wrong understanding affect your relationship with God?

_____

_____

_____

The nature of hell, the final punishment of the wicked, reveals a lot about the character of God. Many have either left Christianity or reject its teachings because they reject the idea of an eternally burning hell. They cannot bring themselves to serve a God who would willingly burn someone for an infinite duration for a finite number of sins. On the other hand, many Christians attempt to use the doctrine of an eternally burning hell to frighten nonbelievers into joining their church. However, Romans 2:4 stresses that it is the "goodness of God," not the fear of hell, that leads a person to genuine and lasting repentance.

Eternal Fire

Officially called "Hell" in 1841, not much is particularly noteworthy about this Michigan town besides its unusual name. Indeed, with winter lows in the teens, it bears little resemblance to the mental image most have of the biblical inferno. So where is the real hell?

Read: Revelation 20:7–9; 2 Peter 3:5–7, 10–13

React: Where is hell located?

_____

_____

_____

Hell is not a mysterious location hidden deep in the earth; rather, it is the earth itself, and all the effects of thousands of years of sin, that will be burnt up and destroyed. This cleansing fire will cover the surface of the whole earth and even into the sky, which has also been polluted by humankind. Once the work is complete, God will create a new earth, one with no stain of sin to mar its incredible beauty.

Read: Matthew 3:11, 12; Jeremiah 17:27; 2 Peter 3:10–13

React: Doesn't the Bible talk about unquenchable fire?

_____

_____

_____

In order to fully understand Matthew 3:11, 12, we must consider other Bible passages that speak on the subject. For instance, Scripture speaks of Jerusalem being destroyed with unquenchable fire, but it is not burning today. It's equally important not to confuse "unquenchable" with "eternal." Unquenchable does not insinuate eternal. By "unquenchable," the Bible means that the fire cannot be put out by human activity. During the destruction of the World Trade Center Towers on 9/11, some journalists described the fire as being "unquenchable"—however, as in the case of Jerusalem, it is no longer burning today.

In Matthew 5:5, the Bible promises that the meek will inherit the earth. We have learned that this cleansing hellfire will burn on earth, but since the earth will someday be the home of the righteous, it is clear that hell cannot burn forever.

Then how long will hellfire burn? The phrase "eternal fire" or "everlasting fire" occurs only three times in the Bible: Matthew 18:8, Mathew 25:41–46, and Jude 7.

Notice two things. First, Matthew 18:8 emphasizes that hell will be a literal place where physical bodies are burned up, not a place consisting of bodiless souls in eternal torment. Second, if you were to travel to the Middle East today, you would find that what were then Sodom and Gomorrah are no longer burning today—even though the Bible references that "eternal fire" destroyed them. This is because the effects of the fire are eternal (people, city destroyed, etc.), even though the fire itself goes out.

Remember Lot's Wife

With no time for goodbyes, she reluctantly began to flee. Her husband hurried her along, but even though her eyes were set on the mountains ahead, her heart remained in the valley behind. Even with the screams and the scorching heat of the blaze on her back—she could resist no longer. "Just one look," she thought. But as Lot's wife turned her face once more to her beloved city, in an instant her body was transformed into a lifeless pillar of salt.

A shocking account, to be sure. Yet Jesus referred back to this incident when He spoke of hellfire and the future destruction of the earth.

Read: Luke 17:29–33

React: What lessons can we learn from Lot's wife?

_____

_____

_____

With compassion in His voice, Jesus urged, "Remember Lot's wife." But tragically, her story will be repeated at the end of the world by millions. Yet it doesn't have to be repeated by us! How easily we can set our eyes toward the Promised Land even as our heart remains in the valley below.

In the midst of this tragic account, Jesus provided hope: "Whoever seeks to save his life will lose it, and whoever loses his life will preserve it" (Luke 17:33). The apostle Paul put it this way: "I have been crucified with Christ; it is no longer I who live, but Christ lives in me; and the life which I now live in the flesh I live by faith in the Son of God, who loved me and gave Himself for me" (Galatians 2:20). If we have died to the influence of the world, then we have no reason to fear the power of death! Ultimately, Jesus will bring us to the saving mountain of life!

Read: Malachi 4:1–3; Psalm 37:10; Psalm 37:20; Matthew 25:41, 46

React: What is the final end of the wicked?

_____

_____

_____

The Bible states that "the wages of sin is death," which is an eternal punishment. (It does not say "eternal punishing," which would denote an ongoing act.) This cleansing of the earth by fire, "hell," was never created for humankind—

only for the devil and his angels. In contrast, God earnestly yearns for each of us to experience His gift of life in Christ!

John 3:16 assures us, "God so loved the world that He gave His only begotten Son, that whoever believes in Him should not perish but have everlasting life." There are only two destinies: to have eternal life or to perish. Consider that if the penalty for sin was eternal torment, then Jesus did not pay for our sins, as Jesus was not tormented eternally. How then could He have paid for the sins of the righteous who will be in heaven if the unrighteous will be burned forever for their sins? Rather, the wages of sin is death—and to be more specific, the second death described in Revelation 21:8. Jesus paid this penalty on the cross when God withdrew from Him completely, causing the Messiah to cry out, "My God, My God, why have You forsaken Me?"

Reflection: Is there anything keeping you from experiencing the peace of full surrender? Is there anything still holding your heart that God is calling you to let go?

The Death of Sin

First Corinthians 15:26 promises that there will come a day when death itself is destroyed. Its gruesome power will finally come to an end!

Read: Romans 6:23; James 1:15; John 3:16, 17

React: What is the ultimate result of sin?

_____

_____

_____

Jesus died to save us from sin, but those who ultimately reject the Author of Life will ultimately receive death, as the final result of sin is death, not everlasting life in hellfire. The wicked "perish," receive "death," while the righteous receive "everlasting life." If the wicked lived forever, being tortured in hell, they would be immortal! But this is impossible because God "alone has immortality" (1 Timothy 6:16). When Adam and Eve were driven from the garden, an angel was posted to guard the tree of life so that sinners could not eat of the tree and, therefore, live forever in their sinful state (Genesis 3:22–24). The teaching that sinners are immortal in hell originated with Satan and is untrue.

Read: Luke 9:56; Isaiah 28:21; Ezekiel 33:11

React: Isn't the act of destroying the wicked contrary to God's nature?

_____

_____

_____

God takes no joy in the death of the unsaved. He yearns for everyone to accept His offer of everlasting life. Destruction by hellfire will break God's heart, because He diligently works to save every soul! But if one spurns His love and clings to sin, God will have no choice but to destroy the unrepentant when He rids the universe of the malignant growth called sin in the fires of the last day.

Read: Revelation 22:12; Matthew 16:27; Luke 12:48

React: Will everyone receive the same reward or punishment at the final judgment?

_____

_____

_____

While we are saved by grace, the Bible says that we will be rewarded according to our works.

Discussion: Who will live in the consuming fire forever? How can we be among these people? Read Isaiah 33:14–16, Hebrews 12:29, and Isaiah 31:9.

_____

_____

_____

Your Questions Answered

Q. Doesn't the story of the rich man and Lazarus in Luke 16:19–31 teach the concept of an eternally burning hell?

A. This story is a parable Jesus used to emphasize a specific spiritual lesson. The point of the story is found in verse 31. Parables should not be taken literally—otherwise, we would believe that trees talk! (See Judges 9:8–15.) Here are some facts making it clear that Luke 16:19–31 is a parable:

1. Abraham's bosom is not heaven (Hebrews 11:8–10, 16).

2. People in hell can't talk to those in heaven (Isaiah 65:17).

3. The dead are in their graves (Job 17:13; John 5:28, 29). The rich man was in bodily form with eyes, a tongue, etc., yet we know from Scripture that the body does not go to hell at death but remains in the grave.

4. People are rewarded at the Second Coming, not at death (Revelation 22:12).

5. The lost are cast into hell at the end of the world, not when they die (Matthew 13:40–42).

The Pharisees viewed earthly wealth as a sign of God's favor. Thus, when Christ told a story about a rich man going to hell while a beggar found comfort in heaven, He was refuting their beliefs and traditions. The Pharisees knew exactly what Christ meant.

Q. Doesn't the Bible talk about being tormented "forever and ever" and "everlasting fire"? (See Matthew 25:41; Revelation 20:7–15; Revelation 14:11; Revelation 20:10.)

A. The term "forever," as used in the Bible, can mean any period of time, limited or unlimited. It is used 56 times in connection with things that have ended. In Jonah 2:6, "forever" means three days and nights. (See also Jonah 1:17.) In Deuteronomy 23:3, "forever" means ten generations. It can also mean "as long as he lives" or "to death." (See 1 Samuel 1:22, 28; Exodus 21:6; Psalm 48:14.) The wicked will burn in the fire as long as they live—in other words, until death.

Sodom and Gomorrah were destroyed with everlasting fire (Jude 7), and that fire turned these ancient cities "into ashes" as a warning to "those who afterward would live ungodly" (2 Peter 2:6). These cities are not still burning today. The fire went out. Likewise, everlasting fire will go out after it has turned the wicked to ashes (Malachi 4:3). The effect of the fire is everlasting, but not the burning itself.

In the end, the devil will also be consumed by fire and turned into ashes. He will not live on for eternity in torment (Ezekiel 28:11–19). Therefore, Revelation 20:10 cannot mean that the devil will burn eternally.

Firm Foundation

"Death is the ultimate penalty for sin. As a result of their sin, all who refuse the salvation God offers will die eternally. But some have sinned flagrantly, demonic in the delight they have taken in causing others to suffer. Others have lived relatively moral, peaceful lives—feeling the effects of guilt mainly because they've rejected the salvation provided in Christ. Is it fair that they suffer the same punishment?

"Christ said, 'the servant who knows the master's will and does not get ready or does not do what the master wants will be beaten with many blows. But the one who does not know and does things deserving punishment will be beaten with few blows. From everyone who has been given much, much will be demanded' (Luke 12:47, 48 NIV).

"Undoubtedly, those who have rebelled against God the most will suffer more than those who have not. But we should understand their ultimate suffering in terms of Christ's 'second death' experience on the cross. There, He bore the sins of the world. And it was the awful separation from His Father that sin brought that caused the agony He suffered—a mental anguish beyond description. So with lost sinners. They reap what they sow not only during this life but in the final destruction. In God's presence, the guilt they feel because of the sins they have committed will cause them to suffer an indescribable agony. And the greater the guilt, the greater the agony. Satan, the instigator and promoter of sin, will suffer the most" (*Seventh-day Adventists Believe*, 2005, p. 413).

Lesson Summary

1. God does not delight in the death of the lost; He longs to save them.
2. The wages of sin is death, not everlasting punishing.
3. The fires of hell will cleanse the earth of sin and all who cling to it.
4. God promises to free us from sin, if we'll let Him, so that we can have the gift of eternal life.

Chapter Eight
THE SECOND COMING

Rescue Mission

In June 1995, Captain Scott O'Grady was flying his F-16 over Bosnia when the fighter jet was cut in two by Serbian anti-aircraft fire. After he ejected and parachuted to the ground, he found himself in a hostile location with the entire Serbian army combing every inch of ground in search of him.

For six days he roamed—cold, wet, tired, hungry, eating bugs, and drinking dirty water. He radioed for help, ran from enemies, and hid under bushes. At times, he had to hide with his face in the dirt to avoid being seen by enemy soldiers passing within a few feet.

Then came a daring rescue from the skies. Forty airships, hundreds of soldiers, and the combined technology of America's armed forces were all engaged to rescue that one lost soldier!

Scott's story still resonates in our day. We are living in hostile territory, and we need deliverance from an enemy. And just like Scott, one day, we will be free from the hurt, hunger, loneliness, and chaos infecting the world. But it's not going to be an earthly army that will deliver us. Soon, Jesus Christ will come ripping through the sky with His angelic host to rescue His children.

But there are many misconceptions regarding how Jesus is actually coming back. So, in this lesson, we'll study what the Bible really says about the greatest rescue mission ever!

Hide Them in Your Heart
Memorize the following verses this week!

"While they looked steadfastly toward heaven as He went up, behold, two men stood by them in white apparel, who also said, 'Men of Galilee, why do you stand gazing up into heaven? This same Jesus, who was taken up from you into heaven, will so come in like manner as you saw Him go into heaven.'" —Acts 1:10, 11

"Let not your heart be troubled; you believe in God, believe also in Me. In My Father's house are many mansions; if it were not so, I would have told you. I go to prepare a place for you. And if I go and prepare a place for you, I will come again and receive you to Myself; that where I am, there you may be also." —John 14:1–3

The Pinnacle of Prophecy

Read: Revelation 1:7; Revelation 22:12, 20

React: With what subject does the book of Revelation open and close? Can we be positive that Jesus will return a second time?

_____

_____

_____

The first words of Revelation tell us what the rest of the book is about. The word "revelation" means "to unveil" or "to reveal." The main focus of this apocalyptic book is to prepare humanity for the ultimate revelation of Christ, which will be His second coming.

In Matthew 26:64, Jesus testified that He would come back to the earth. Since the Scriptures cannot be broken (John 10:35), this is proof positive that He will return. It is Christ's personal guarantee! Moreover, Jesus fulfilled the prophecies of His first coming, so we can be certain that He will fulfill the prophecies concerning His second coming as well!

Read: John 14:1–3; Revelation 19:6–10; Matthew 25:1–13

React: What is the purpose of Jesus' second coming? What symbolism does Jesus use to describe His return? How can we be ready to meet Him when He comes?

_____

_____

_____

Using the symbol of marriage, Jesus paints a touching picture of what His return is all about. When a Jewish man in His day proposed to a woman, he would leave her for a period of time with the promise of a soon return. His focus would then be on preparing a place for her in his father's house. After his work was finalized, he would return to reunite with his bride and bring her to his home. The bride would anticipate her groom's return, not knowing the day of his coming. The groom's arrival was announced by a shout, which alerted the bride.

Reflection and Discussion: "The promise of Christ's second coming was ever to be kept fresh in the minds of His disciples. The same Jesus whom they had seen ascending into heaven, would come again, to take to Himself those who here below give themselves to His service. The same voice that had said to them, 'Lo, I am with you alway, even unto the end,' would bid them welcome to His presence in the heavenly kingdom" (*The Acts of the Apostles*, pg. 33).

Raptured Away

The Bible says that before Jesus comes again, Satan will impersonate Him. To pave the way, the devil has presented a strong delusion to the Christian world—a deception that has almost unanimously been accepted in most denominations. It is sometimes called the "secret rapture," and it teaches that Christ's return will be quiet and unseen as His people are snatched away to heaven.

Read: Acts 1:9–11; Revelation 1:7; Matthew 24:27, 30; 1 Thessalonians 4:16

React: How many will see Jesus return? Will it be something people can miss?

_____

_____

_____

Will there be a rapture? Yes! The word "rapture" simply means "to be carried away with power." But the rapture of God's people will not be a secret event! Many teach that the return of Christ will take place quietly, but the Bible teaches that when Jesus comes, every one of our senses will be bombarded with the evidence of His coming. No one will miss it happening!

Read: 1 Corinthians 15:51–53; 1 Thess. 4:16, 17; 2 Thess. 2:8; Philippians 3:20, 21

React: What will happen to the righteous and the wicked when Jesus comes? Will Jesus touch the earth?

_____

_____

_____

According to the Bible, the dead in Christ will rise and the believers who are alive at His coming will join them to meet Jesus "in the air." The living who refused to repent will perish from His radiant glory.

Thus, God's people shouldn't be fooled by any news that says Christ is in Paris, Times Square, Moscow, or anywhere else on the earth. False christs will appear on the earth and even do miracles (Matthew 24:23–27), but Jesus will remain in the clouds above the earth at His second coming.

Reflection and Discussion: What do you look forward to most about the Second Coming?

_____

_____

_____

Even at the Door

How close is the return of Jesus? The Bible describes the condition of the world just before this event. Some signs include:

- Pervasive unrest, fear, upheaval, disasters, and war — Luke 21:9, 25, 26
- Moral degeneracy and a craze for pleasure — 2 Timothy 3:1–5
- Unbelief and scoffers — 2 Peter 3:3; 2 Timothy 4:3, 4
- Lawlessness — Matthew 24:12; 2 Timothy 3:13; Ezekiel 7:23
- Rampant spiritualism — 1 Timothy 4:1; Revelation 16:14

React: Is it important for Christians to understand what's happening in the world around us? Does seeing these signs fulfilled create a desire in you to tell more people to get ready for Jesus' return?

_____

_____

_____

What are some other signs of Jesus' return?

- Jesus predicted the destruction of Jerusalem in Matthew 24:2, 16; this was fulfilled in AD 70 when Rome attacked the city.
- Jesus also predicted a religious tribulation in verse 21. More than 50 million believers were martyred for their faith during the Dark Ages.
- In Daniel 12:4, we're told that the world would experience an unprecedented increase in knowledge and ability to travel.
- Jesus also said that prior to His return, the message of the gospel would be heard around the world (Matthew 24:14). This is being fulfilled today!

While we cannot know the day or the hour of Christ's return (Matthew 24:36), we *can* know that His coming is near. One practical takeaway to knowing that Jesus' return is near is to question whether or not our hearts are ready for Him.

Reflection and Discussion: Knowing that upheaval will soon grip the world, how can you balance the sharing of these vital truths without causing someone to fear?

_____

_____

_____

Preparation for the Day

As people living in our troubled times reflect on the world's rising evils and the increasing reality that a major disaster or conflict will occur at some point in their lives, many have become "survivalists." Also called "preppers," such people are now building bunkers, stockpiling food, and hoarding other resources in the hope that they'll be ready to survive natural disasters, terrorist attacks, or even global nuclear war. The question is—will such measures truly save anyone?

Read: Luke 21:36; Colossians 4:2; 1 Peter 4:7; Matthew 5:14–16

React: What is the most important preparation for the Second Coming?

_____

_____

_____

Wilderness lookouts spend their summers in towers surrounded by forests. During the dry seasons, their job is to continually watch for wildfires caused by careless campers or lightning strikes. They stay in constant radio communication with firefighters to save lives.

Likewise, rather than focusing on our own survival, Christians should be a light to the world. To do so in an age of fear and unrest, we must maintain a vibrant relationship with the Lord. A strong prayer life and Bible study are the most important components in surviving last-day events and Satan's deceptions before being reunited with Jesus.

Read: Matthew 4:4; Job 23:12; John 3:5; Mark 13:33–37

React: How important is it to have the Bible's promises stored in our hearts? At a time when our senses are bombarded by smartphones, TVs, games, and gadgets, how do we keep our eyes on Christ?

_____

_____

_____

As you wait for Jesus to return, He wants to prepare you for living in the eternity to come. To help you do this, He has promised to "put My laws in their mind and write them on their hearts" (Hebrews 8:10).

Your Questions Answered

Q. Wasn't Jesus speaking of a "secret rapture" in Luke 17:36?

A. No. Instead, Jesus was describing end-time world conditions that are similar to Noah's Flood and the destruction of Sodom (Luke 17:26–37). He told how God spared Noah and Lot and destroyed the wicked. He said specifically that the flood and fire "destroyed them all" (vv. 27, 29). In each case, a few were taken to safety and the remaining were destroyed. Then He added, "Even so will it be in the day when the Son of Man is revealed" (v. 30). To illustrate, Jesus said, "Two men will be in the field: the one will be taken and the other left" (v. 36).

There is nothing secret about His return. "Every eye will see Him" (Revelation 1:7). At His second coming, Christ publicly and openly takes the righteous up into the clouds (1 Thessalonians 4:16, 17), while His holy presence slays the wicked (Isaiah 11:4; 2 Thessalonians 2:8). That's why Luke 17:37 speaks of the bodies of the wicked. (See also Revelation 19:17, 18.) The wicked who are left behind at Christ's coming are left dead.

Q. When will Christ set up His kingdom on the earth?

A. After the thousand-year period of Revelation 20. This millennium begins at the Second Coming—when Jesus takes the righteous from earth to heaven to live and reign with Him for "a thousand years" (Revelation 20:4). At the close of the one thousand years, "the holy city, New Jerusalem" (Revelation 21:2) comes down from heaven to the earth with all the saints (Zechariah 14:1, 5). The wicked dead of all ages are then raised to life (Revelation 20:5). They surround the city to capture it (Revelation 20:9), but fire comes down from out of heaven and devours them. This fire purifies the earth and burns up all traces of sin (2 Peter 3:10; Malachi 4:3). Then God creates a new earth (2 Peter 3:13; Isaiah 65:17; Revelation 21:1) and gives it to the righteous, and "God Himself will be with them and be their God" (Revelation 21:3). Perfect, holy, happy beings, restored once again to the perfect image of God, will at last be at home in a sinless world—just as God originally planned!

Firm Foundation

"When the time came for Christ to ascend to His Father, He led the disciples out as far as Bethany. Here He paused, and they gathered about Him. With hands outstretched in blessing, as if in assurance of His protecting care, He slowly ascended from among them. 'It came to pass, while He blessed them, He was parted from them, and carried up into heaven'" (*The Acts of the Apostles*, p. 32).

"Thus will be fulfilled Christ's promise to His disciples, 'I will come again, and receive you unto Myself' (John 14:3). Those who have loved Him and waited for Him, He will crown with glory and honor and immortality. The righteous dead will come forth from their graves, and those who are alive will be caught up with them to meet the Lord in the air" (ibid., p. 34).

Lesson Summary

1. The Second Coming is the climactic event of Scripture.
2. There will be a rapture, but it won't be a secret.
3. We should share the good news of His soon coming with the world.
4. The signs of His coming are fast fulfilling.
5. God desires all His children to be ready when He comes.
6. We have to be ready ourselves before we can help others prepare.

Chapter Nine
THE SABBATH, PART 1

The Law of God

As crime and violence overrun our cities and homes, doesn't it make more sense than ever for every citizen to obey the laws of the land in order to secure the peace and safety? These laws were made to protect people living in a sinful world.

Likewise, our heavenly Father cares deeply for humanity's safety, and He has been trying to protect us with His laws. Go back to one of the most earth-shaking events in history: when God spoke His moral law from Mount Sinai. The Ten Commandments are so important to God, He bypassed proclaiming them through a prophet and spoke them Himself: "God spoke all these words" (Exodus 20:1).

Yet He did more than just speak His commandments; He wrote them with His finger onto tablets of stone. Have you ever wondered why? "My covenant I will not break, nor alter the word that has gone out of My lips" (Psalm 89:34). God was saying that there is an unchangeable quality to His law, yet many believe that the Ten Commandments were, in fact, changed—or "done away with." But how can that be when Jesus, the voice of God on earth, said, "It is easier for heaven and earth to pass away than for one tittle of the law to fail"? (Luke 16:17).

Thus, our goal in this week's lesson is to see what Scripture says about the relevance of God's Ten Commandments for His people today.

Hide Them in Your Heart
Memorize the following verses this week!

"Then God blessed the seventh day and sanctified it, because in it He rested from all His work which God had created and made." —Genesis 2:3

"So He came to Nazareth, where He had been brought up. And as His custom was, He went into the synagogue on the Sabbath day, and stood up to read." —Luke 4:16

The Law of Liberty

Read: James 1:25; Romans 13:10; John 14:15; Matthew 5:17, 18

React: How can a law that restricts behavior be called "a law of liberty"? What one word summarizes God's law?

_____

_____

_____

God's law is like a road map; it points out the right path to lasting happiness. "By the law is the knowledge of sin" (Romans 3:20). "I would not have known sin except through the law. For I would not have known covetousness unless the law had said, 'You shall not covet'" (Romans 7:7).

Did you also know that in Scripture, God and His law are described with the same characteristics? Notice the following:

	God is ...	The law is ...
Good	Luke 18:19	1 Timothy 1:8
Holy	Isaiah 5:16	Romans 7:12
Perfect	Matthew 5:48	Psalm 19:7
Pure	1 John 3:2, 3	Psalm 19:8
Just	Deuteronomy 32:4	Romans 7:12
True	John 3:33	Psalm 19:9
Spiritual	1 Corinthians 10:4	Romans 7:14
Righteousness	Jeremiah 23:6	Psalm 119:172
Faithful	1 Corinthians 1:9	Psalm 119:86
Love	1 John 4:8	Romans 13:10
Unchangeable	James 1:17	Matthew 5:18
Everlasting	Genesis 21:33	Psalm 111:7, 8

It could even be said that the moral law is God's character in written form; the Ten Commandments help us to better comprehend the Lord. And because God is love, we can know that the Ten Commandments can be summarized by the word love. Moreover, it is no more possible to change God's law than to change God.

Read: Romans 3:20, 31; 1 John 3:4; Ephesians 2:8, 9

React: What is the Bible's definition of sin? Can anyone be saved by keeping the law? If not, what is the purpose of the law?

_____

_____

_____

Salvation comes only through grace, as a gift of Jesus Christ, and we receive this gift by faith, not as a payment for our good works. Rather, the law functions as a mirror that points out the sin in our lives. Just as a mirror can show you the dirt on your face but cannot be used to clean your face, so cleansing and forgiveness from sin come only through Christ.

The Covenants

Read: Exodus 19:4–8

React: What did God promise the Israelites if they obeyed His commandments? How did the people respond?

_____

_____

_____

   Israel self-confidently entered into a special relationship with God; unfortunately, Bible history affirms that they failed again and again in keeping their end of the agreement—often referred to as the "old covenant."

   Many Christian teachers have said that the problem with this covenant was in the law itself, which is why, they say, Jesus came to do away with the law. But as we have learned, God's law is like God Himself: It is both perfect and unchangeable. So what actually went wrong with the old covenant if it wasn't God or His law?

Read: Proverbs 3:1–3; Jeremiah 31:33; Ezekiel 36:26, 27; Hebrews 8:7–13

React: What are the similarities and differences between the old and new covenants? What are the better promises in the new covenant?

_____

_____

_____

   Many are surprised to learn that the new covenant still requires that God's people obey the Ten Commandments. The moral law still stands for believers today as strongly as it did for the people of ancient Israel. So what is the actual difference between the two covenants?

   The book of Hebrews reveals that the old covenant collapsed because it was partially based on the faulty promises of a people with stony hearts. (See Hebrews 8:8, 9.) However, the new covenant rests entirely on the faithful promises of a perfect, unfailing God—who promises to recreate people by writing His very law into their hearts, turning hearts of stone into hearts of flesh.

Reflection and Discussion: Some people fear that since God still expects obedience today, they are no longer saved when they fall. But Romans 5:20 explains, "Where sin abounded, grace abounded much more." This promise is rooted in the changeless, perfect God who is willing to provide you not only with complete forgiveness, but also with all the power necessary—through His Holy Spirit—to help you overcome every temptation in your life to break His law, as long as you are willing to let Jesus into your heart. Is this your desire today? Explain:

_____

_____

_____

The Sabbath Question

Read: Genesis 2:1–3; Exodus 16:22–31; 20:8–11; Deuteronomy 5:15

React: When did the Sabbath originate? Why do you think God starts the fourth commandment with the word "remember"?

_____

_____

_____

God created the Sabbath at the time of Creation; the Bible says that He "blessed and sanctified" the seventh day. Sanctified means "made holy." This means that the seventh day was set aside for a special purpose not at Mount Sinai, as many believe, but at the dawn of humanity—before sin existed on earth and thousands of years before the Hebrew nation was formed.

The Sabbath serves as a memorial to humanity of God's work of creation. When the Lord "rested," it did not mean that He needed to take a break because He was fatigued. Rather, it means that He had finished the work of creating the physical world. His "resting" was an example to humans to stop working on the seventh day, not only to recover from our labors, but also as a time to connect with God in a special way.

Just as God set an example for us to rest on the seventh day, we are also to follow the example of Jesus who kept the Sabbath "as His custom" (Luke 4:16). Notice also that in Matthew 24:20, Jesus referred to the Sabbath as still being the Sabbath long after He departed the earth.

Read: Acts 13:13, 14, 42–44; 17:2; 18:4; Hebrews 4:9

React: What did New Testament believers do in regard to the Sabbath?

_____

_____

_____

While Jesus came to fulfill the law, does that mean He "set aside" or "did away with" the fourth commandment for future believers? There is no evidence that Jesus' followers stopped observing the Sabbath after His death and resurrection.

In fact, as the young church grew, the apostles not only continued keeping the Sabbath holy, they also taught Gentiles to honor it. This includes the apostle Paul, who implored Jews not to burden Christian Gentiles with Hebrew customs. Why? Because Paul understood that "the Sabbath was made for man," not just the Jews! (See Mark 2:27, 28.)

Reflection and Discussion: Isaiah 66:22, 23 reveals that even after God creates the new heavens and the new earth, humans will still be observing the Sabbath. This is powerful evidence that the Sabbath and God's law will stand forever!

War Against the Sabbath Commandment

Read: Revelation 12:17

React: How does Satan feel about the Sabbath and other commandments?

_____

_____

_____

It is Satan's constant goal to convince people that God's law no longer matters, and he actively makes war on those who keep God's commandments.

Satan especially hates the Sabbath, because it also serves as a sign of our redemption. (See Ezekiel 20:12.) Just as the Israelites were delivered from their cruel taskmasters in Egypt, so also God saves us from the bondage of sin and the power of Satan through the lifegiving grace of Jesus Christ, who died on the cross to save us from sin and death.

Just as the Lord made the seventh day holy, God wants to make His people holy—free from sin. The Sabbath is a precious gift to humanity, and the enemy wants to keep that gift in darkness.

Read: Matthew 11:28; 1 John 5:3; Revelation 14:7, 12; 22:14

React: Why is the Sabbath an important issue in these last days?

_____

_____

_____

Did you know that one of the three proclamations of the three angels includes a direct reference to the Sabbath commandment? "The Lord made the heavens and the earth, the sea" (Exodus 20:11). This tells us that the Sabbath will have been forgotten by many of God's people at the end of time—but that His messengers will once again restore it in the hearts of believers before Jesus returns.

Why? Because people who love God will want to keep His commandments. It is not a burden to keep the Sabbath day; in fact, it is a joy that brings healing and peace to those who seek to obey God.

Reflection and Discussion: Maybe you are familiar with the Sabbath yet haven't been faithful in keeping it holy. God has asked His people to stop trampling on His holy day (Isaiah 58:1, 13, 14). Do you accept this invitation, and will you commit to sharing this message with others in a Christ-like manner?

Your Questions Answered

Q. Isn't it little more than legalism to keep the Sabbath or any of the commandments?

A. It is no more "legalistic" to avoid adultery than it is to keep the Sabbath. Law and grace do not work in competition but in cooperation. The law, including the Sabbath, points out our sin, and grace empowers us to overcome sinful desires and deeds. "For this is the love of God, that we keep His commandments. And His commandments are not burdensome" (1 John 5:3).

Q. It seems that according to Romans 14:5, the day we keep is a matter of personal opinion—isn't it?

A. Romans chapter 14 talks about a particular problem in the early Christian church in which some believers were judging other believers in regard to their observance of annual Jewish feasts found in the ceremonial law. (See the next question for more on this.) Thus, the issue here is not the seventh-day Sabbath, which is a part of the moral law. The apostle Paul was warning Christians to avoid judging others for not observing feast days as they did.

Q. Doesn't Colossians 2:14–17 do away with the seventh-day Sabbath?

A. Not at all. It refers only to the sabbaths that were "a shadow of things to come" and not to the seventh-day Sabbath.

There were seven yearly holy days in ancient Israel that were also called "sabbaths." These were in addition to, or "besides the Sabbaths of the LORD" (Leviticus 23:38)—that is, the seventh-day Sabbath. These other sabbaths foreshadowed, or pointed to, the cross and ended at the cross. God's seventh-day Sabbath was made before sin entered our world, and therefore could not foreshadow about deliverance from sin. That's why Colossians chapter 2 differentiates the sabbaths that were "a shadow." The seven yearly sabbaths that were completed at the cross are listed in Leviticus chapter 23.

Firm Foundation

Baptist: "There was and is a commandment to keep holy the Sabbath day, but that Sabbath day was not Sunday. … It will be said, however, and with some show of triumph, that the Sabbath was transferred from the seventh to the first day of the week. … Where can the record of such a transaction be found? Not in the New Testament—absolutely not. There is no scriptural evidence of the change of the Sabbath institution from the seventh to the first day of the week" (Dr. Edward T. Hiscox, author of *The Baptist Manual*).

Catholic: "You may read the Bible from Genesis to Revelation, and you will not find a single line authorizing the sanctification of Sunday. The Scriptures enforce the religious observance of Saturday, a day which [Catholics] never sanctify" (James Cardinal Gibbons, *The Faith of Our Fathers*).

Church of Christ: "We have the testimony of Christ on this subject. In Mark 2:27, he says: 'The Sabbath was made for man, and not man for the Sabbath.' From this passage it is evident that the Sabbath was made not merely for the Israelites, … but for man. … Hence we conclude that the Sabbath was sanctified from the beginning, and that it was given to Adam, even in Eden, as one of those primeval institutions that God ordained for the happiness of all men" (Robert Milligan, *Scheme of Redemption*).

Episcopal: "Sunday … was adopted by the early Christians as a day of worship. … No regulations for its observance are laid down in the New Testament, nor, indeed, is its observance even enjoined" ("Sunday," *A Religious Encyclopedia*, Vol. 3).

Presbyterian: "Until, therefore, it can be shown that the whole moral law has been repealed, the Sabbath will stand. … The teaching of Christ confirms the perpetuity of the Sabbath" (T. C. Blake, D.D., *Theology Condensed*).

Pentecostal: "Why do we worship on Sunday? Doesn't the Bible teach us that Saturday should be the Lord's Day? … We will have to seek the answer from some other source than the New Testament" (David A. Womack, *The Pentecostal Evangel*).

Lesson Summary

1. God's law of love is a transcript of His character.
2. His "law of liberty" is designed to protect humanity from the bondage of sin.
3. Obedience is part of the old and new covenants; it's the promises that are different.
4. The Sabbath was instituted at Creation and will be kept throughout eternity.
5. Satan hates the Sabbath because it symbolizes Jesus' redemption and re-creation.

Chapter Ten
THE SABBATH, PART 2

The Seal and the Mark

The Great Seal of the Realm is the royal signet of Great Britain and Northern Ireland. It has been in use for nearly ten centuries, through more than a dozen monarchs and even a rumored dunking in the River Thames. It remains one of the most prized and meticulously protected possessions in the United Kingdom. The seal even has its own bodyguard: the Lord Chancellor. In order to ensure its authenticity, only one mold of the seal exists at a time.

Every seal has three key components: a name, a title, and a territory. For example, the Great Seal currently bears these words: "Elizabeth II, by the Grace of God, of the Britains and her other realms, Queen, Head of the Commonwealth of Nations, Defender of the Faith." A seal signifies someone's authority over a given territory, and to forge a seal is considered a terrible crime of deception.

Well, did you know that God has His own seal? No, it's not a signet ring or a stamp. It is something far more precious: the Sabbath day. In this study, we will learn more about the Sabbath and about another seal that stands against it—the mark of the beast.

Hide Them in Your Heart
Memorize the following verses this week!

"It is a sign between Me and the children of Israel forever; for in six days the Lord made the heavens and the earth, and on the seventh day He rested and was refreshed." —Exodus 31:17

"Here is the patience of the saints; here are those who keep the commandments of God and the faith of Jesus." —Revelation 14:12

The Beast from the Sea

Before exploring the mark of the beast, we must first determine what the beast is. We find the answer in Revelation 13—but studying Revelation also inevitably means studying the book of Daniel. The two go hand in hand prophetically, as questions posed in Daniel are often answered in Revelation. Whereas the book of Daniel "seal[s]," or conceals, understanding (Daniel 12:4), Revelation reveals (Revelation 22:10).

Read: Revelation 13:1, 2; Daniel 7:3–8, 17, 23

React: How is the sea beast connected to the prophecies in Daniel?

_____

_____

_____

The sea beast is a composite beast, made up of the three beasts from Daniel 7. These three beasts represent the three kingdoms that in turn dominated the then-known world: Babylon (symbolized by the lion), Medo-Persia (bear), and Greece (leopard). The sea beast came to power *after* the other three and implemented traditions and practices derived from these previous kingdoms. In this way, the sea beast in Revelation parallels the fourth beast of Daniel 7. A study of Daniel 2 and history affirms this beast as Rome.

Read: Revelation 13:1–10, 15–18

React: What are some of the identifying characteristics of the beast from the sea?

_____

_____

_____

The sea beast has at least ten important characteristics listed in Scripture, including rising from a heavily populated area (represented by the sea; see Revelation 17:15), having global authority (Revelation 13:3, 7), and being led by one man (v. 18). While the previous three kingdoms were primarily political in nature, the sea beast takes on a religious element—it receives worship (vv. 4, 8), is blasphemous (vv. 1, 5, 6), and persecutes God's saints (v. 7). These identifying characteristics make it clear that the sea beast is also parallel to the little horn power of Daniel 7, which grew out of the fourth beast. Only the system of

Roman Catholicism, the papacy, which grew out of pagan Rome, satisfies all ten requirements. (For more about this link, see the Amazing Facts *Storacles Lessons* #13 and #14.)

Who Will You Worship?

Read: Revelation 13:4, 8; Daniel 7:25; Isaiah 14:12–14; Ezekiel 28:2, 6, 18

React: Who is the enabling power behind the sea beast? What motivations are at work in the sea beast's attack against God's followers?

_____

_____

_____

    The devil is the empowering force behind the sea beast (the dragon is a symbol for the devil; see Revelation 12:9). He has been warring against God and His law since he first spread rebellion in heaven. He wants God's throne. For the devil, it has always been about stealing the worship that rightfully belongs to God.

Read: Revelation 13:5–7, 16, 17; Daniel 7:7, 19, 21, 23, 25

React: What is the devil's government like?

_____

_____

_____

    The devil's government is one of force and violence.
    Through the papacy, the devil has set up a counterfeit to God's government. While it looks similar to God's government, its principles are diametrically opposed. For example, the sea beast blasphemes God (Revelation 13:6). In the Bible, blasphemy is claiming to be God or claiming to forgive sins as God would (John 10:33; Luke 5:21). Catholic priests offer to pardon sins, while the pope claims to be the "Vicar of Jesus Christ."
    Additionally, the little horn (Daniel 7's equivalent to the sea beast) sought to "change times and law" (Daniel 7:25). Though the Bible promises that God does not change, the papacy claims the authority to change the Ten Commandments. In addition to omitting the second commandment and dividing the ninth into two, they've also altered the fourth commandment—the only commandment dealing with time: "The Church of God has in her wisdom ordained that the celebration of the Sabbath should be transferred to 'the Lord's day'" (*Catechism of the Council of Trent*, p. 3).

Reflection and Discussion: When studying the end-time beast power, why is it important to remember Jesus' statement in John 10:16?

_____

_____

_____

The Seal of God

At the end of time, all people on the earth will be separated into two groups: those who worship the beast and those who worship God. All people will receive a mark that indicates whom they've chosen to worship.

Read: Revelation 14:9–12; Ezekiel 9:4–6; Revelation 12:17; Revelation 7:3

React: What are the differences between God's seal and the beast's mark?

_____

_____

_____

God's mark, or seal, is about faithfully obeying His commandments, not out of mere duty but out of love. That is why God's followers, His "saints," are marked only in their foreheads. They have purposed in their hearts to love, honor, and obey Him (Hebrews 10:16). The fruit, their good works, is a natural extension of what is in their hearts.

Read: Exodus 20:8–11; Exodus 31:16, 17; Ezekiel 20:12, 20; Revelation 14:7

React: Why is the Sabbath commandment singled out as God's mark?

_____

_____

_____

Laws and seals go hand in hand. A seal authenticates, approves, and binds a law. Remember from day one of this week's study the Great Seal of the Realm and its three key components? The name identifies the owner of the seal, the title proves the owner authority, and the territory shows the reach of that authority.

Well, God's Sabbath commandment is the only commandment of the ten that has those three key components. It states His name as "Lord," His title as our Creator, and the territory He rules: "heaven and earth, the sea, and all that in them is." The Sabbath commandment is not just an arbitrary day. It is the day that defines when God created our world. It is a day that eternally binds us, His creation, to Him.

The mark of God, His seal, His "sign," is the Sabbath commandment.

The Mark of the Beast

Read: Revelation 13:8, 16, 17; Revelation 14:9–11

React: What is the mark of the beast?

_____

_____

_____

The mark of the beast is a seal that defines the devil's government. Contrary to popular opinion, the mark is not a literal mark, like a tattoo or a bar code. Instead, it's the mark of the devil's government, which seeks to counterfeit God's government. Since the Sabbath is the seal that symbolizes God's government, it follows that the counterfeit day of worship the Catholic Church has instituted is the mark of the beast. Sunday worship is the mark of the beast.

Read: Revelation 14:6–12

React: Summarize the three angels' messages in Revelation 14. Why are they important today?

_____

_____

_____

The three angels' messages are God's words to all people. They reveal what will happen to the two groups of people at the very end of time, and they give each of us the freedom to choose between the two groups.

The devil knows that he has but a short time (Revelation 12:12). He, the arch deceiver, has forged fake worship in order to deceive millions to follow him. His rebellion and terrible lies have sealed his fate. But our destiny is still a matter of choice! "Choose for yourselves this day whom you will serve" (Joshua 24:15).

The messages of the three angels define God for who He truly is—and the devil for who he truly is. They are a revelation, a warning, and a call. In these last days, this is the message we as Christians take to the world, crying aloud, "Make a stand for God, our Creator, our Redeemer, our King!"

Your Questions Answered

Q. What is the "Lord's Day"?

A. "The Lord's Day" is a phrase found only once in the Bible, in Revelation 1:10. It is commonly interpreted to be Sunday, the day most Christians go to church. However, there is no indication in Scripture that "the Lord's Day" is Sunday. In fact, there is scriptural evidence to the contrary. In three of the Gospels, Jesus refers to Himself as Lord of the Sabbath (Matthew 12:8; Mark 2:28; Luke 6:5). Given Christ's own declaration, it stands to reason that "the Lord's Day," as it is stated in Scripture, refers to the seventh-day Sabbath or Saturday—not Sunday.

Q. Do people have the mark of the beast now?

A. No. Until keeping Sunday as holy is enforced by law—until the Catholic Church makes it illegal and punishable to work on Sunday—no one has the mark of the beast. There is a choice that everyone must make, whether for God or for the dragon. No one is forced against his will to make this decision, but ultimately everyone chooses one side or the other and receives a mark: "No one can serve two masters; for either he will hate the one and love the other, or else he will be loyal to the one and despise the other. You cannot serve God and mammon" (Matthew 6:24). The question still remains: Whom do you serve?

Firm Foundation

"The third angel's message has been sent forth to the world, warning men against receiving the mark of the beast or of his image in their foreheads or in their hands. To receive this mark means to come to the same decision as the beast has done, and to advocate the same ideas, in direct opposition to the word of God. ... If the light of truth has been presented to you, revealing the Sabbath of the fourth commandment, and showing that there is no foundation in the word of God for Sunday observance, and yet you still cling to the false Sabbath, refusing to keep holy the Sabbath which God calls "My holy day," you receive the mark of the beast. When does this take place?—When you obey the decree that commands you to cease from labor on Sunday and worship God, while you know that there is not a word in the Bible showing Sunday to be other than a common working-day, you consent to receive the mark of the beast, and refuse the seal of God. If we receive this mark in our foreheads or in our hands, the judgments pronounced against the disobedient must fall upon us. But the seal of the living God is placed upon those who conscientiously keep the Sabbath of the Lord" (*Review & Herald*, July 13, 1897).

Lesson Summary

1. The sea beast is both pagan and papal Rome, analogous to the fourth beast (Rome) and little horn power (papacy) of Daniel 7.

2. The Sabbath represents God's character by His name as Lord of all, by His title as Creator, and by His territory of heaven and earth.

3. Everyone has a choice to make as to whom he or she will worship, and that choice will determine his or her eternal destiny.

4. Those keeping the seventh-day Sabbath to love and honor God show they belong to God—they have His seal in their forehead.

5. Those who keep Sunday sacred, refusing to honor God, will receive the mark of the beast.

Chapter Eleven
STEWARDSHIP

The Gift of You

Clara Hale was affectionately known as "Mother Hale" for good reason. She fostered forty children, cared for community kids during the Great Depression, found families for homeless children, taught parenting classes, and cared for more than a thousand drug-addicted babies through the Hale House Foundation. Up to her death at age 87, she kept at least one infant in her own room. Mother Hale gave herself generously to the cause that inspired her.[1]

Her daughter Lorraine did not. After Clara's death, Lorraine took over the charity's management. Using donor money, she spent $444,953 on a statue of her mother and $440,133 on an art collection for her office. Her husband was heard calling the children "cash cows"—and it's no wonder, since Lorraine used over $1 million for personal gain: a jacuzzi, theatrical production, a brother's legal costs, and personal property taxes.[2]

While Clara was a model of generosity, Lorraine was a model of selfishness. Instead of using the funds as donors intended, Lorraine squandered them on herself. The Bible says that we are also responsible for funds that are not our own. What kind of stewards will we choose to be? Like Lorraine, we can use our time, talents, and money to serve ourselves. Or, like Clara, we can give them to God's cause.

This week, we'll look at the role that stewardship plays in the Christian life.

Hide Them in Your Heart
Memorize the following verses this week!

"'Bring all the tithes into the storehouse, that there may be food in My house, and try Me now in this,' says the Lord of hosts, 'If I will not open for you the windows of heaven and pour out for you such blessing that there will not be room enough to receive it.'" —Malachi 3:10

"Whatever you do, do it heartily, as to the Lord and not to men, knowing that from the Lord you will receive the reward of the inheritance; for you serve the Lord Christ." —Colossians 3:23, 24

---

1   https://en.wikipedia.org/wiki/Clara_Hale
2   https://www.charitywatch.org/charitywatch-articles/charitywatch-hall-of-shame/63

A Matter of the Heart

Read: Psalm 24:1; 50:10–15; 1 Chronicles 29:10–14

React: How did David and Asaph respond to God's ownership of the world and all that's in it? What are the implications for our own response to God's ownership and enabling?

_____

_____

_____

    Stewardship is more about the heart than the money! When we recognize God as the ultimate owner and see our wealth and abilities as gifts from the Creator, our hearts begin to shift from greed to gratitude. Instead of pride over our work, possessions, and self-sufficiency, we find humility and dependency on the God who made the universe.

Read: Matthew 6:24–33

React: How should we as Christians conduct our lives so it's clear to others who we serve?

_____

_____

_____

    Contrast these promises of Jesus with the experience of God's people in Haggai's day:

"You have sown much, and bring in little; you eat, but do not have enough; you drink, but you are not filled with drink; you clothe yourselves, but no one is warm; and he who earns wages, earns wages to put into a bag with holes" (Haggai 1:6).

    The Israelites had put their own houses first, leaving God's temple in ruins. They made the startling discovery that putting their needs first was like storing their money in a bag filled with holes.

    How much better it is to recognize God as owner, put His righteousness first, and stand back to watch how He meets our needs!

Reflection and Discussion: What does it look like to "seek the kingdom of God and His righteousness"? How has God met your needs while you were busy serving Him?

_____

_____

_____

Investing in Your Future

Read: Malachi 3:6–12

React: How does the Lord reward those who bring their tithes to His storehouse?

_____

_____

_____

The word "tithe" means one-tenth; thus, tithing is the practice of returning a tenth of our increase to God as a reminder that the other nine-tenths also belong to Him. Just as financiers turn small amounts of money into larger amounts through wise investments, God is offering to exchange a tenth of our income for overflowing blessings!

Read: Nehemiah 13:4–13

React: In Nehemiah's day, where were the tithes received and what was their purpose? What are the modern-day equivalents?

_____

_____

_____

Today's church uses tithe to support its mission of sharing the message of Jesus, paying its evangelists, pastors, and conference leaders. But while it may seem that leadership is receiving and spending our tithe, the real storehouse is in heaven: "Here mortal men receive tithes, but there he receives them, of whom it is witnessed that he lives" (Hebrews 7:8). When we return our tithe to the earthly church, Jesus receives it in His heavenly storehouse. Tithing is one of many ways to "lay up for yourselves treasures in heaven." Remember, wherever your treasure is, "there your heart will be also" (Matthew 6:21).

Reflection and Discussion: In Malachi chapter 3, God says that not tithing is the same as robbing Him. Despite this, less than ten percent of all U.S. Christians give ten percent of their incomes.[3] What obstacles to tithing exist in your life? How do these obstacles hold up in light of God's promises?

_____

_____

_____

---

3   Christian Smith and Michael O. Emerson, *Passing the Plate: Why American Christians Don't Give Away More Money* (New York: Oxford University Press, 2008).

Love's Multiplication

Read: 2 Corinthians 8:1–9

React: What does the apostle Paul say about the believers in Macedonia? What impresses you about their example?

_____

_____

_____

In addition to tithe, many Christians enjoy giving an additional offering. The values of our hearts are sometimes expressed through our wallets. The Macedonian believers first gave themselves to God, but then they quickly followed that up with sacrificial gifts to help church members in Jerusalem who were suffering a famine. Paul's words here echo Christ's lesson in Luke 7:43–48: Those who are forgiven much, love and give much. Those who do not realize the extent to which they have been forgiven and are not grateful for it, love and give little.

Psalm 96:8 encourages us, "Give to the Lord the glory due His name; bring an offering, and come into His courts." Our offerings are one way to express our gratitude to God and to give Him glory for what He's done in our lives.

Read: 2 Corinthians 9:6–15

React: How much should we give in offering?

_____

_____

_____

Paul outlines several results of the generous giving he encourages. God is able to provide for the needs of the givers! Their daily needs will be met (v. 8). Also, God can multiply their gifts, making them more impactful (v. 7). And because of their gifts, God will receive thanksgiving from those who are helped; when they see how Christians have "confessed the gospel" through their giving, they glorify God.

When we give our offerings joyfully, with love for others and gratitude for God in our hearts, the results are multiplied many times over!

Time, Talent, and Eternity

Read: Psalm 37:18; 39:4, 5; 90:10–12; 91:16

React: What contrasting truths about time are presented in these psalms?

_____

_____

_____

People often lament, "I don't have enough time!" Of course, no one has time for everything, but even our time should be seen as a gift from God. And He doesn't give insufficient gifts! We *do* have enough time; what we need is the wisdom to spend it well. Indeed, that our days on earth are limited helps us to focus on what's truly important! Reflecting on his frailty, King David concluded, "Lord, what do I wait for? My hope is in You" (Psalm 39:7). While we wait for our eternal inheritance, wise management of our time includes spending time with God in prayer, avoiding time wasters, and focusing on what's truly important both in this life and in eternity.

Read: 1 Peter 4:7–11

React: What activities does the apostle Peter consider to be good uses of our time? What does he consider to be wise stewardship of our gifts and talents?

_____

_____

_____

Our gifts are not our own! Peter says that good stewards use their gifts in ministry for others. But this doesn't happen through their own natural ability; we only minister through Christ's enabling. And this process brings glory to Jesus!

We're instructed, "Whatever you do, do it heartily, as to the Lord and not to men, knowing that from the Lord you will receive the reward of the inheritance; for you serve the Lord Christ" (Colossians 3:23, 24). Instead of using our abilities for ourselves, we should use them in God's service. As we do, He will both enable and reward us!

Reflection and Discussion: What are some unique ways that we as Christians today can be good stewards of our time? What obstacles stand in our way and how do we overcome them?

_____

_____

_____

Your Questions Answered

Q. I don't like how my church is using my tithe. Can I instead pay tithe to those who will use it in the way I think it should be used?

A. Leviticus 27:30 emphasizes that tithe is not ours: "All the tithe of the land, whether of the seed of the land or of the fruit of the tree, is the LORD's. It is holy to the LORD." Because it doesn't belong to us, where it's returned and how it's used isn't up to us. Our job is simply to give God's tithe back to Him—and to trust Him to take care of it. God is well able to take care of any who misuse what belongs to Him.

Q. My finances are so tight, I can barely give anything. What should I do?

A. In Mark 12:41–44, Jesus calls the disciples' attention to the miniscule gift of a widow. She shyly dropped two mites into the temple treasury. A mite was the smallest coin in circulation at that time—just 1/128th of a day's wages for the typical day laborer.[4] Yet this is what Jesus said of her gift: "Assuredly, I say to you that this poor widow has put in more than all those who have given to the treasury; for they all put in out of their abundance, but she out of her poverty put in all that she had, her whole livelihood." Our gifts are measured by the level of our sacrifice and the attitude of our heart. Jesus is pleased with our gifts of love and sacrifice, no matter their size!

4   Dybdahl, Jon L, editor. *Andrews Study Bible: Light. Depth. Truth.* Andrews University Press, 2010. Mark 12:42

Firm Foundation

"Christians should heed the command, 'Bring ye all the tithes into the storehouse, that there may be meat in Mine house' (Malachi 3:10). If professing Christians would faithfully bring to God their tithes and offerings, His treasury would be full. There would then be no occasion to resort to fairs, lotteries, or parties of pleasure to secure funds for the support of the gospel.

"He whose heart is aglow with the love of Christ will regard it as not only a duty, but a pleasure, to aid in the advancement of the highest, holiest work committed to man—the work of presenting to the world the riches of goodness, mercy, and truth.

"It is the spirit of covetousness which leads men to keep for gratification of self means that rightfully belong to God, and this spirit is as abhorrent to Him now as when through His prophet He sternly rebuked His people, saying, 'Will a man rob God? Yet ye have robbed Me. But ye say, Wherein have we robbed Thee? In tithes and offerings. Ye are cursed with a curse: for ye have robbed Me, even this whole nation' (Malachi 3:8, 9).

"The spirit of liberality is the spirit of heaven. This spirit finds its highest manifestation in Christ's sacrifice on the cross. ... The principle there illustrated is to give, give. 'He that saith he abideth in Him ought himself also so to walk, even as He walked' (1 John 2:6).

"On the other hand, the spirit of selfishness is the spirit of Satan. The principle illustrated in the lives of worldlings is to get, get. Thus they hope to secure happiness and ease, but the fruit of their sowing is misery and death.

"Not until God ceases to bless His children will they cease to be under bonds to return to Him the portion that He claims. Not only should they render the Lord the portion that belongs to Him, but they should bring also to His treasury, as a gratitude offering, a liberal tribute. With joyful hearts they should dedicate to the Creator the first fruits of their bounties—their choicest possessions, their best and holiest service. Thus they will gain rich blessings. God Himself will make their souls like a watered garden whose waters fail not" (*The Acts of the Apostles*, pp. 338, 339).

Lesson Summary

1. Stewardship of our money, time, and talents is a heart issue that recognizes God's ownership and is a practical demonstration of our trust in God.

2. Tithe belongs to God and should be returned to the church.

3. God promises to reward faithful tithing with even more blessings.

4. Our offerings express gratitude and love; God multiplies their impact.

5. Through God's enabling, good stewards use their time and talents in service to others.

6. Our time on earth is limited to help us focus on what's most important, but part of our Christian reward is enjoying eternity!

Chapter Twelve
STRENGTH

Your Body a Temple

In 2013, Irv Gordon of Long Island set a world record with his classic sportscar. His feat? Reaching the 3,000,000-mile reading on the odometer of his 1966 Volvo P1800S Coupe. Most cars only go a fraction of that distance before reaching their final destination—the junkyard.

So what was Irv's secret? He lovingly cared for the Volvo, never pushing the 1.8L 4-cylinder engine too hard, reading the owner's manual carefully, sticking strictly to the maintenance regimen, taking it in for oil changes every 3,500 miles, and replacing worn-out components with genuine parts from the manufacturer. Amazingly, the engine had to be rebuilt just twice in all those miles.

Our bodies are well-designed machines—millions of times more complex than a car or any other human invention—and capable of incredible feats. We, too, have an owner's manual, though not very many people take the time to search out and follow the Inventor's recommendations.

But does it matter? Is physical health really *that* important to our spiritual lives and to our relationship with God? Could better health even enhance our witness to others? Let's prayerfully study the Bible's answers this week!

Hide Them in Your Heart
Memorize the following verses this week!

"Do you not know that your body is the temple of the Holy Spirit who is in you, whom you have from God, and you are not your own? For you were bought at a price; therefore glorify God in your body and in your spirit, which are God's." —1 Corinthians 6:19, 20

"Therefore, whether you eat or drink, or whatever you do, do all to the glory of God." —1 Corinthians 10:31

Something Better

Read: 3 John 1:2

React: Why do you think God is concerned with our physical health?

_____

_____

_____

Genesis 1:26 says that we are made in the image of God. As such, we are His children, and what parent doesn't want his or her children to be healthy? The Lord wants to spare us the bodily suffering that afflicts much of the world. Additionally, He created us for a high purpose—to mirror His love to other people. We were created "for good works" (Ephesians 2:10), and we need strong bodies in order to best carry out that purpose.

Note that our minds, spiritual natures, and bodies are closely linked. If our body isn't functioning well, our thinking will be impaired to some degree. Since the mind, the "heart" in Scripture, is where we connect with God, how we care for our bodies can affect our spiritual lives.

Read: Exodus 15:26

React: From where does true healing come? What is the natural result of obedience to God's health laws?

_____

_____

_____

The closer we can live to God's ideal for us, the better our health will tend to be. Although we live in a polluted, sinful world with many genetic and environmental factors outside our control, following the health principles found in Scripture will help us maximize our potential for good health.

Reflection and Discussion: Read Proverbs 4:20–22. Why is it important to carefully search for God's wisdom when regaining or maintaining our health?

_____

_____

_____

As our Creator, God knows exactly what we need to thrive—and He wants to help us! By observing His health laws, we can reap the more abundant life Jesus wants us to experience.

The Recipe for Health, Part One

Millions in our world suffer from chronic diseases that are, in most cases, avoidable and preventable. Every day, we make dozens of choices that affect our health for better or worse. During the next two days, we'll look at some biblical health principles that can guide us to healthier choices.

Read: Genesis 1:29; Deuteronomy 14:6, 9; Leviticus 11:13–44

React: What was humanity's original diet? What animals does God state are unfit for humans to eat?

_____

_____

_____

Remember, these aren't arbitrary rules; there are solid scientific reasons behind them. God understands in intricate detail the nature of every creature He has made, and He knows what diet is best for each one. If we love Him, we will trust in His wisdom and gladly keep His health laws (John 14:15).

Read: Proverbs 20:1; Proverbs 23:31, 32

React: What does the Bible say about alcoholic drinks, and what does this imply about other harmful substances?

_____

_____

_____

In 1 Corinthians 3:16, 17, we are warned against defiling our bodies, which is the holy temple of God. Alcohol, tobacco, and illicit drugs can significantly damage our health. This, in turn, can weaken us spiritually. That's why we're cautioned to "abstain from fleshly lusts which war against the soul" (1 Peter 2:11). We should guard against anything that compromises our health and, instead, rely on God for strength to abandon our destructive habits. "I can do all things through Christ who strengthens me" (Philippians 4:13).

Reflection and Discussion: Read Daniel 1:8–19. What were Daniel and his friends concerned about as they considered the food and drink offered to them?

_____

_____

_____

These young men chose not to defile themselves with the wine, unclean meat, and rich foods that were urged upon them. As a result, they excelled in intelligence and were rewarded with high positions in the government.

The Recipe for Health, Part Two

Read: Genesis 3:19; Psalm 127:2; Mark 6:31

React: Why is it important to balance our activity and rest? How did Jesus guide His disciples into this balance?

_____

_____

_____

Exercise and other physical activities are important, especially in our culture. These days, many people sit at a desk for most of the day and manual labor is more uncommon than in the past. The Bible confirms that exercise certainly has some value (1 Timothy 4:8), but it also points out the necessity of proper sleep and rest.

Read: Genesis 2:3; Exodus 20:9, 10; Ezekiel 20:12

React: What has God provided that is critical to a right relationship with Him and essential to optimum health and strength?

_____

_____

_____

Even before sin entered our world, God gave us the Sabbath as a time to rest and seek a deeper relationship with Him. Jesus kept the Sabbath (Luke 4:16; Matthew 12:8), as did His disciples after He returned to heaven (Acts 13:14, 44; 16:13). This law, highlighted with a "remember" in the heart of the Ten Commandments, was intended to bless humanity for all time.

Here are some of the other health laws found in the Bible:

Health Principle	Bible Text
1. Eat at regular intervals and don't eat animal fat or blood.	Ecclesiastes 10:17; Leviticus 3:17
2. Avoid overeating.	Proverbs 23:2
3. Don't envy others or hold grudges.	Proverbs 14:30; Matthew 5:23, 24
4. Be happy and cheerful.	Proverbs 17:22
5. Trust in the Lord.	Proverbs 19:23
6. Keep yourself clean.	Isaiah 52:11
7. At mealtimes, enjoy yourself.	Ecclesiastes 3:13
8. Help those in need.	Isaiah 58:6–8
9. Be temperate.	1 Corinthians 9:25

A Better Tomorrow

Read: Malachi 4:2; Romans 8:23

React: What will God ultimately do for those who belong to Him?

_____

_____

_____

At Jesus' second coming, all those who belong to Him will receive new bodies that are completely healthy and strong. Scripture says we will be changed instantly at His return: "For this corruptible must put on incorruption, and this mortal must put on immortality" (1 Corinthians 15:53). By His grace and power, we will be equipped to live eternally!

Read: Revelation 21:1–4; Isaiah 35:6

React: What does Scripture say life will be like in the new earth?

_____

_____

_____

In our current world, nearly everyone will at some point suffer from sickness, disease, or injury in their lives. Though many are sick because of poor lifestyle choices, others are ill through no fault of their own. The innocent suffer on a regular basis. But the Bible says it will not always be this way.

Though now we can hardly imagine a world without injury or illness, eventually God will recreate our planet. He assures us, "They shall not hurt nor destroy in all My holy mountain, for the earth shall be full of the knowledge of the LORD as the waters cover the sea" (Isaiah 11:9). Furthermore, "the inhabitant will not say, 'I am sick'" (Isaiah 33:24).

If you struggle with health challenges, or know someone who does, take hope in God's promises for the future. While we should do everything in our power to live healthfully in the here and now—whatever the results, we can be sure of a brighter tomorrow when we will be made whole.

Your Questions Answered

Q. First Timothy 4:4 says, "Every creature of God is good, and nothing is to be refused." Doesn't this mean we can eat whatever we want?

A. This Scripture passage is referring to foods "which God created to be received with thanksgiving" (v. 3) by His people. These foods are the clean foods listed in Leviticus 11 and Deuteronomy 14. Verse 4 of this passage makes it clear that all creatures of God are good and not to be refused, provided they are among those created to be "received with thanksgiving" (clean animals).

Verse 5 reveals why these animals (or foods) are acceptable: They are "sanctified" by God's Word, which says they are clean, and by a "prayer" of blessing, which is offered before the meal.

Q. Isn't it enough to simply love the Lord and not concern ourselves with His health laws?

A. If you truly love the Lord, you will be eager to obey His health laws because that's the way He has designed for you to achieve optimal health, happiness, and purity. "He became the author of eternal salvation to all who obey Him" (Hebrews 5:9). Jesus said, "If you love Me, keep My commandments" (John 14:15). When we truly love the Lord, we won't try to dodge His health laws or His commandments or make excuses. This attitude actually reveals the true heart in the other things of God. "Not everyone who says to Me, 'Lord, Lord,' shall enter the kingdom of heaven, but he who does the will of My Father in heaven" (Matthew 7:21).

Firm Foundation

"God's laws, which include the laws of health, are not arbitrary but are designed by our Creator to enable us to enjoy life at its best. Satan, the enemy, wants to steal our health, our joy, our peace of mind, and ultimately to destroy us (see John 10:10)" (*Seventh-day Adventists Believe*, Second Edition, p. 313).

"To the first couple, the Creator gave the ideal diet: 'I give you every seed-bearing plant on the face of the whole earth and every tree that has fruit with seed in it. They will be yours for food' (Genesis 1:29 NIV). After the Fall, God added to their diet 'the plants of the fields' (Genesis 3:18 NIV). Today's health problems tend to center on the degenerative type of diseases directly traceable to diet and lifestyle. The diet God planned, consisting of grains, fruits, nuts, and vegetables, offers the right nutritional ingredients to support optimum health.... The distinction between clean and unclean animals dates back to Noah's day—long before Israel existed. As principles of health, these dietary laws carry with them an ongoing obligation" (ibid., pp. 317, 319).

"Drugs have saturated our society because they offer stimulation and release from stress and pain. The Christian is surrounded with seductive invitations to use drugs. Even many innocent-appearing, popular beverages contain drugs. Coffee, tea, and colas contain caffeine, and fruit-flavored wine coolers contain alcohol. Research has shown that the milder gateway drugs tend to lead progressively to stronger mind-altering drugs. The wise Christian will abstain from all that is harmful, using in moderation only that which is good. ... Since God communicates with us only through our minds, it is well to remember that alcohol adversely affects their every function" (ibid., pp. 314, 315).

Lesson Summary

1. God wants us to enjoy an abundant life.
2. Scripture gives us guidelines to avoid harming our health.
3. The Sabbath is an essential part of balancing activity and rest.
4. God will ultimately bring healing to His people.

Chapter Thirteen
SPIRIT OF PROPHECY

Finding His Prophets

We've all seen the news: Infamous cult leaders receiving special messages from "God"—announcing prophecies about terrifying future events, engaging in bizarre religious ceremonies, and sometimes even leading to the untimely deaths of their devoted followers.

Perhaps that's why, in our modern world, the word "prophet" puts even the least skeptical among us on edge. Yet the Bible does predict that there will be prophets working in the last days. Indeed, it is one of the signs of Jesus' coming.

In Revelation 12:17, the devil is described as being enraged with the faithful, those "who keep the commandments of God and have the testimony of Jesus Christ." Revelation 19:10 defines this "testimony of Jesus," a characteristic of God's last-day movement, as being "the spirit of prophecy." The outpouring of His Spirit, as revealed through dreams and prophecies, is promised to occur before He comes.

But how can we differentiate the genuine prophet from the false one? How can we be receptive to messages that are truly being sent from God without risking fatal deception? This week, we'll explore the biblical answer and learn how to decipher between the true and the false for ourselves.

Hide Them in Your Heart

Memorize the following verses this week!

"Surely the Lord God does nothing, unless He reveals His secret to His servants the prophets." —Amos 3:7

"To the law and to the testimony! If they do not speak according to this word, it is because there is no light in them." —Isaiah 8:20

"Do not quench the Spirit. Do not despise prophecies. Test all things; hold fast what is good." —1 Thessalonians 5:19–21

Can You Hear Me?

Read: Genesis 3:8; Isaiah 59:2

React: How did God communicate with Adam and Eve before sin entered the world? How does sin affect our connection to Him today?

_____

_____

_____

Before sin entered the world, the Lord spoke to Adam and Eve in person; they were privileged to enjoy being in His physical presence. This was God's original plan for us, and this level of intimate communion is what God is working to restore through His plan of salvation.

Sin now separates us from God and prevents us from communicating with Him directly in physical form. It is not a lack of willingness on God's part, but an inability on our part to stand in His presence that prevents God from physically revealing Himself to us.

Read: Romans 2:15; Hebrews 1:1, 2; Amos 3:7

React: How does God communicate with humankind today?

_____

_____

_____

God communicates with us through His Word, through our consciences, through the person of Christ, and through His prophets. Whenever God has wanted to send a clear message to His people, He most often chose to use a prophet. God's most direct way of communication is through prophets. If the people rejected a prophet, "there was no remedy" left for them (2 Chronicles 36:16).

Reflection and Discussion: If we are limited by sin from communicating with God directly, how is it that certain people (prophets) are still able to communicate with Him in this way? (See Matthew 5:8.)

_____

_____

_____

The degree to which God reveals Himself to a person depends on that person's purity of heart. When we are living in conscious rebellion to God, we are not able to discern His voice clearly. However, if we repent of our sins and turn from our wicked ways, our connection with God is restored. As we continue to live in accordance with His will, we hear God's voice more clearly.

119

What's in a Name?

Read: Exodus 7:1, 2; Isaiah 30:9, 10; 1 Samuel 9:9

React: Is the role of a prophet simply to predict the future?

_____

_____

_____

In Scripture, the term "prophet" is utilized to describe a spokesman or speaker, as in the case of Aaron. Contrary to popular belief, a prophet is not someone who merely foretells the future. Prophets are also referred to as "seers" because they are the eyes of God's church and God used the messages given them to open the eyes of the church. Just as our bodies need eyes to see, the body of Christ needs prophets for its spiritual vision (Proverbs 29:18).

Read: Revelation 12:17; Revelation 19:10; Matthew 24:11, 24; Joel 2:28–31

React: Will the prophetic gift be seen in the last days?

_____

_____

_____

If there were to be no true prophets during the time of the end, Christ could have simply warned against anyone even claiming that gift. But His warning against false prophets implies that there will indeed be true prophets. The signs and wonders recorded in Joel chapter 2 clearly point to the time of Christ's second coming, confirming that these dreams and prophecies will occur just prior to the end of the world (Matthew 24:29).

Reflection and Discussion: What are some of the ways in which God speaks to prophets? (See Numbers 12:6–8.)

_____

_____

_____

It is crucial to note that simply because someone says they had a dream or vision from God, it does not make it true. For instance, God will not contradict Himself; thus, His Word can be used to test every prophecy. "To the law and to the testimony! If they do not speak according to this word, it is because there is no light in them" (Isaiah 8:20).

Keeping the Body Intact

Imagine if a friend walked up to you, calmly pointed at your face, and stated, "Look! A nose!" While you might question the sanity of your friend, it would not surprise you to know that there is, indeed, a nose on your face.

But imagine that this same friend walked toward you, pointed at the ground, and said, "Look! A nose!" Might you be concerned? While a nose is a normal attribute of the body, finding it dismembered would indeed be alarming!

The same idea is true about the body of Christ. First Corinthians 12 paints a beautiful picture of the body of Christ, emphasizing how crucial and intricately connected each member is to the whole.

One of the gifts given to the church is the gift of prophecy (Ephesians 4:11). Removing this gift from the church would be to dismember the body.

Read: Ephesians 4:11–13

React: Why is the prophetic gift given to the church? How long will it remain?

_____

_____

_____

While it's easy to accept that prophets existed "way back then," it can be more challenging to accept it in our time. However, Jesus addressed this very issue during His earthly ministry. (See Matthew 23:29–32). If God sends a prophet, it is because there is something He wants to tell His people.

We might ask, "If the Bible is sufficient for salvation, what need do we have now for a prophet?" Consider the example of John the Baptist. When John came on the scene, he did not add anything to the Scriptures. The truth behind his preaching could already be found in those Scriptures. But John played a crucial role in preparing the way for Christ's first advent by expounding on truths that were not properly understood in his time. He stressed the urgency and nearness of the Messiah's coming. God often sent prophets to His people as a catalyst for revival.

Reflection and Discussion: How do we test a prophet to know whether or not he or she is from God?

_____

_____

_____

Fulfilled predictions are one of the tests of the prophets (Jeremiah 28:9). However, note these two important points: First, some prophecies are conditional (Jeremiah 18:7–10; Jonah 3:10). Second, some prophecies from false prophets also come true (Deuteronomy 13:1–4; 2 Corinthians 11:13–15).

Applying the Test

Read: 1 Thessalonians 5:19–21; 2 Chronicles 20:20

React: How should we respond to prophecy? What is promised to those who believe God's prophets?

_____

_____

_____

In December 1844, a group of young Methodist women were kneeling in prayer in Portland, Maine, when 17-year-old Ellen Harmon (White, after she married) received her first vision. As she faithfully and urgently related what God had revealed to her, she continued receiving visions and dreams for about 70 years, until her death in 1915.

As was true for many biblical prophets, certain supernatural phenomena accompanied Ellen during her visions. Like the prophet Daniel, she did not breathe while in vision and often lost physical strength (Daniel 10:8, 17). Some of her visions lasted as long as four hours, but she did not breathe the entire time, according to physician examinations.

At other times, Ellen was given supernatural strength (Daniel 10:18, 19). Though she weighed only 95 pounds, witnesses saw her hold a 17-pound family Bible in her outstretched hand for 30 minutes while in vision. These and other phenomena indicate that there was something supernatural about her experience; however, they do not tell us whether this prophet was from God or Satan. Thus, when faced with a supernatural claim to the prophetic gift, Christians must test the claim by the Bible to see if it is true.

Amazing Facts About the Ministry of Ellen G. White

- She wrote 5,000 articles and 26 books
- She is the most translated woman writer in the history of literature and the most translated American author of either gender (in more than 148 languages).
- Her writings cover a broad spectrum of topics, including education, health, prophecy, nutrition, cultural and ethnic-linguistic issues, and creationism.
- From the age of 17 until her death, she received approximately 2,000 visions and dreams.

Your Questions Answered

Q. In Bible days, was the gift of prophecy limited to men?

A. No. In addition to the many men who had the gift of prophecy, God also gave the gift to at least eight women: Anna (Luke 2:36–38); Miriam (Exodus 15:20); Deborah (Judges 4:4); Huldah (2 Kings 22:14); and the four daughters of Philip, an evangelist (Acts 21:8, 9).

Q. What are the Bible qualifications for a true prophet?

A. The Bible's testing points to know whether a prophet is from God include:

1. Lives a godly life (Matthew 7:15–20)
2. Was called to service by God (Isaiah 6:1–10; Jeremiah 1:5–10; Amos 7:14, 15)
3. Speaks and writes in harmony with the Bible (Isaiah 8:19, 20)
4. Predicts events that come true (Deuteronomy 18:20–22)
5. Has visions (Numbers 12:6)
6. Physical evidences during vision, such as supernatural strength, weakness, and lack of breath (Daniel 10:18, 19; Daniel 10:8, 17)

Q. Do true end-time prophets originate new doctrine, or does doctrine come strictly from the Bible?

A. True end-time prophets do not originate doctrine (Revelation 22:18, 19). The Bible is the source of all doctrine. However, true prophets do:

1. Lead God's people into a closer walk with Jesus
2. Help God's people understand difficult, unclear, or unnoticed portions of the Bible so that they come to life for us and bring great joy
3. Help protect God's people from fanaticism, deception, and spiritual stupor
4. Help God's people understand end-time prophesies
5. Help God's people sense the certainty of Jesus' soon return

Q. If we believe "the Bible and the Bible only," shouldn't we reject modern-day prophets?

A. The Bible is the sole source of Christian doctrine. However, the same Bible points out: The gift of prophecy will exist in God's church until the end of time (Ephesians 4:11, 13; Revelation 12:17; 19:10; 22:9). To reject a prophet's counsel is to reject God's will (Luke 7:28–30). We are commanded to test prophets and follow their counsel if they speak and live in harmony with the Bible (1 Thessalonians 5:20, 21). Thus, people who base their faith on "the Bible only" must follow its counsel regarding prophets. True prophets will always speak in harmony with the Bible. Prophets who contradict God's Word are false and should be rejected. If we fail to listen to and test prophets, however, we are not basing our faith upon the Bible.

Firm Foundation

Ellen White and the Bible

Ellen White was a firm believer in the Scriptures and referred to them as the greater light. "The word of God is the great detector of error; to it we believe everything must be brought. The Bible must be our standard for every doctrine and practice. We must study it reverentially. We are to receive no one's opinion without comparing it with the Scriptures. Here is divine authority which is supreme in matters of faith. It is the word of the living God that is to decide all controversies" (*The Ellen G. White 1888 Materials*, pp. 44, 45).

Contributions to Health and Medicine

Ellen White's teachings regarding health were at least one hundred years ahead of her time and have only recently been substantiated by science.

For instance, during her time, tobacco was considered medicinal. But she wrote, "Tobacco is a slow, insidious, but most malignant poison. In whatever form it is used, it tells upon the constitution; it is all the more dangerous because its effects are slow and at first hardly perceptible. It excites and then paralyzes the nerves. It weakens and clouds the brain" (*Ministry of Healing*, pp. 327, 328).

She also wrote, "Grains, fruits, nuts, and vegetables constitute the diet chosen for us by our Creator. These foods prepared in as simple and natural a manner as possible are the most healthful and nourishing" (*Ministry of Healing*, p. 296). The medical community has only recently recognized the same: "Vegetarians have been shown to have greater longevity, superior muscular endurance, less chronic diseases, less utilization of health care facilities including hospitals, and less need for medications" (Dr. Neil Nedley, *Proof Positive*, p. 540).

While this introduction to the prophetic nature of Ellen White's ministry is by no means conclusive, it provides us with the opportunity to become noble Bereans and to "search the Scriptures to see whether these things are so." (See Acts 17:11.)

Lesson Summary

1. God communicates with us through His Word, through our consciences, through the person of Christ, and through His prophets.

2. Prophets are God's most direct form of communication.

3. One of the gifts given to the church is the gift of prophecy.

4. God will not contradict Himself; His Word must test all prophecies.

5. While God uses prophets to reveal the future, they also draw His people into closer communion with Him.

The Amazing Facts App:
The Bible truth in your pocket!

Download Amazing Facts' free mobile app today and put the ministry's most essential resources at your fingertips!

You'll get fact access to ...

- AFTV 24-hour television
- Amazing Facts Internet Radio
- All our audio and video archives
- Daily devotional messages
- Free book library
- Study Guides
- Ministry news
- Our weekly current events blog
- And more!

Download the app now!
Available for iOS and Android

Amazing Facts
Bible Study Guides

If you or your church is searching for the perfect tool to share your faith with family, friends, neighbors, or entire communities, nothing beats the fully updated, redesigned Amazing Facts Bible Study Guides! These 27 information-packed topical lessons have already led thousands to embrace the last-day message of Jesus Christ!

Item: SG-CBLK

Titles include:
- Is There Anything Left You Can Trust?
- Did God Create the Devil?
- Rescue from Above
- Who Is the Antichrist?
- Keys for a Happy Marriage
- Written in Stone
- The USA in Bible Prophecy
- and many more

Get yours now for your personal witnessing needs
or as part of a church-wide outreach effort!

Visit afbookstore.com
or call 800-538-7275!

Have you been called to witness but don't know what to do or even where to start?

Amazing Disciples

Our informative and inspiring quarterly lesson book will empower your outreach and help you become a confident disciple of Christ!

Created by the Amazing Facts Center of Evangelism team , this unique lesson book features 13-weeks of powerful keys to transformative witnessing—including personal preparation, giving Bible studies, answering objections, and much more!

Item: AF-AD

Amazing Disciples Teachers Edition

And if your church is looking to empower the witness of all your members, you'll love the comprehensive teachers edition of *Amazing Disciples,* which provides easy-to-follow teaching guidance, expert advice, sample lesson plans, and other tools you need to help others become enthusiastic and effective soul winners for Christ.

Item: BK-ADTE

Visit afbookstore.com or call 800-538-7275!